The Shared Memories Of

....

Grandparents & Grandchildren

Shared Memories

BY

CAROL ABRAMS & FERNE MARGULIES

General Publishing Group

Publisher: W. Quay Hays
Editorial Director: Peter L. Hoffman
Art Director: Chitra Sekhar
Editor: Dana Stibor
Production Director: Trudihope Schlomowitz
Prepress Manager: Bill Castillo
Production Assistants: Tom Archibeque, David Chadderdon, Gus Dawson, Russel Lockwood, Bill Neary, Regina Troyer
Copy Editor: Carolyn Wendt
Editorial Assistance: Kristi Cardarella

For information:
General Publishing Group, Inc.
2701 Ocean Park Boulevard, Suite 140
Santa Monica, CA 90405

Library of Congress Cataloging-in-Publication Data
Abrams, Carol.
    Grandparents & grandchildren : shared memories / by Carol Abrams
and Ferne Margulies.
        p.   cm.
    ISBN 1-57544-076-8 (hardcover)
    1. Grandparents—Case studies.   2. Grandchildren—Case studies.
3. Grandparent and child—Case studies.   4. Grandparent and child—
-Pictorial works.   I. Margulies, Ferne.   II. Title.
HQ759.9.A27   1998
306.874'5—dc21   98-9573
                                                                                    CIP

Printed in the USA by RR Donnelley & Sons Company
10 9 8 7 6 5 4 3 2 1

General Publishing Group
Los Angeles

Table of Contents

In loving memory of my maternal grandparents, Tillie and Samuel Schor. And to my mother, Leonore Kelvin, who was a "grand" parent long before she became a grandmother.

-Carol Abrams

For my maternal grandmother, Bessie Mold, who gave me her inner strength and unconditional love.

-Ferne Margulies

Introduction

Several years ago when her grandfather died, my daughter, Tracy, commented wistfully, "No one will ever smile at me again the way that Poppy did." Her bittersweet lament was both touching and illuminating. For although Tracy had been brought up thousands of miles away from her paternal grandparents, and had infrequent visits with them and little in common with their everyday lives and interests, she nevertheless believed with absolute certainty in her grandfather's unparalleled love.

I recalled Tracy's remark on the afternoon that Ferne Margulies and I met for the first time. We were meeting at the suggestion of a mutual friend who believed we would make good collaborators. Prepared to dazzle each other with our creative ideas, Ferne and I lunched at a Los Angeles outdoor café. The energy in this "power lunch" hot spot was palpable, but after an hour and a half—and several rounds of decaffeinated coffee—the two of us still hadn't gotten around to discussing business. Instead, in the process of learning about each other, Ferne and I had settled into talking about our first love and our most creative endeavor—our families.

At the time, neither of us had married children, let alone grandchildren, but we both confessed that the possibility of one day becoming grandparents thrilled us. We'd witnessed the elation of our friends who were already in that enviable role, and were promised by them, "It's the best experience ever!" Since grandparents today can look forward to increased longevity and vitality and being companions to their grandchildren well into the latter's adult years, Ferne and I consoled ourselves, agreeing that we still had time! Then, in short order, we found ourselves segueing to a related topic: reminiscing about our own grandparents and the relationships we'd had with them.

Ferne is luckier than I am, retaining vivid memories of an adored grandmother—her *Bubba*. "On Sunday mornings," Ferne recalled fondly, "my mother would take me to Bubba's apartment in Santa Monica. The halls always smelled of chicken soup or brisket and there was the 'chop chop' sound of someone making chopped liver. My grandmother always called me by my Jewish name. 'So, Fagel,' she'd say, 'how was your week?' I would go on and on and she would listen as though there were nothing more important in the entire world. She never rushed me. If her phone rang she would tell my mother, 'I'll call them back. Tell them I'm with my granddaughter.' Bubba was like a safe harbor filled with love. I could curl up on her lap and her big, thick arms would envelop me. I never gave it a second thought—I always just knew I was loved."

Memories of my grandparents are hazier, but no less filled with love. My maternal grandmother had a devastating stroke when I was very young, but I can remember how her eyes shone when I sat by her bed and held her hand, or performed a song I'd heard on the *Hit Parade*. And I can picture her husband, my Grandpa Sam, a waiter who toiled endlessly in noisy, smoke-filled restaurants but who nevertheless delighted in having his 12 grandchildren assemble around his holiday dining room table where he'd serve us as if we were really big tippers! An enlargement of their wedding picture—a serious-faced, sepia-toned formal portrait of an incredibly young-looking bride and groom—hangs in my office. I like to think that they're looking over me.

Ferne and I realized that everything we were talking about—the joy of our own friends who had become grandparents and the heartfelt memories that we had as grandchildren—was not unique. What was unique was the unforgettable, irreplaceable bond between grandparents and grandchildren. Suddenly we knew that this was a subject we wanted to explore together, and *Grandparents & Grandchildren: Shared Memories* was launched.

What began on that sunlit patio café has turned into an experience richer and deeper than anything we could have imagined. Over the past two years, Ferne and I have had the good fortune to be welcomed into the homes and hearts of grandparents and grandchildren around the country. We have been awed by octogenarians able to recall their own grandparents in startlingly vivid detail; grandchildren who admit they relate to their grandparents in a way that they can't with their parents; grandparents who confess that grandparenting gives them "a second chance to do it right"; and grandchildren who'd rather "hang out" with their grandparents than do just about anything else. From each person we met, the youngest to the oldest, we learned something of value and were touched and enriched forever. We are deeply appreciative for their kindness and candor, and regard each as special, adding his or her own original element to the mix.

As you read on, you will discover that some of the grandparents and grandchildren share the same name, facial features, preferences, values, beliefs, and abilities. A few live around the corner from each other and enjoy daily visits; others conduct their relationship via telephone and e-mail from homes across the country. Many have taken family vacations together; some have made the emotional journey back to family homelands and roots. Sporting events, sleepovers, storytelling, and mutual hobbies are part of the shared joy, as are holidays when memorable gifts are exchanged and favorite recipes savored.

But whatever the disparity in experiences, one universal theme runs through all the relationships we encountered: The grandparents and grandchildren we talked with love each other unconditionally. There is an absence of the expectation, rivalry, and tension that exists in parent/child and sibling relationships. It's been said that grandparents love their grandchildren "just because they're breathing." One young granddaughter confirmed this, describing her grandfather's feelings for his grandchildren as "He's just glad we were born!"

As you get to know the special people highlighted on the following pages, our hope is that you will not only enjoy sharing in their memories and experiences, as we did, but also find yourself recalling some of your own.

Carol Abrams
March 1998

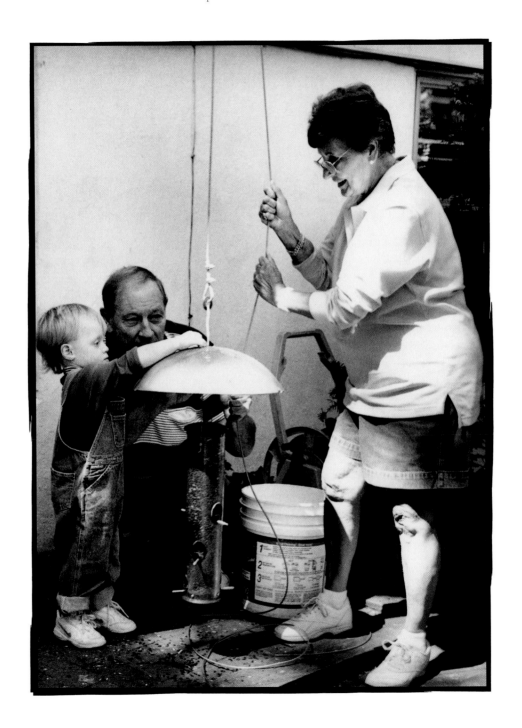

Harry

Joan Gamble

Tommy Gamble

*T*acked to a kitchen wall in his New Jersey home is a newspaper clipping about Harry Gamble—the football coach, the man, the grandfather. The article's headline, which probably caused more than a few double takes, reads:

HARRY GAMBLE RETIRES FROM NFL TO SPEND MORE TIME WITH GRANDSON

An unusual sports-page story? Indeed. But then, Harry Gamble is an unusual man!

In early 1997, the former general manager and president of the Philadelphia Eagles was an executive with the National Football League in New York City. His long days started with a wake-up alarm at 5:10 A.M., then a two-hour-and-15-minute rush-hour train ride into Manhattan. After a busy eight-hour day, he'd head home, facing another two hours and 15 minutes gone from his life.

At the same time, Gamble's wife and perennial cheerleader, Joan, happily spent a lot of her time at home caring for their grandson. "I had begun watching Tommy several days a week while his parents went to work," says Joan. "I love doing it! Maybe it's because I have more patience and more time than I did when our boys were young. I'm also more confident, knowing that I did a good job, because we have such great kids."

Harry, meanwhile, was missing out on the grandparenting experience. "Every morning, when I'd leave for work, I'd call out to Joan, 'Try and keep Tommy up so I can see him tonight,'" says Gamble. "Then one morning, I'm sitting on the train riding into the city, and it hits me. I'm Tommy's grandfather, and he's the only grandchild I have. He's only going to be little for a brief period of time, and I'm missing it. This child is getting away from me. I ought to be spending my total time, or a whole lot more of it, with him, my sons, and their families. I realized that I had my priorities all screwed up."

"I've always loved horticulture," Gamble says. A big teddy-bear-of-a-man, better known for his winning record on the field than for his green thumb, Gamble and his landscape architect son, Harry Jr., have turned a suburban backyard into an outdoor wonderland where the former coach can share the joys of nature with Tommy.

When the energetic toddler runs into the yard to join his grandparents, Gamble instinctively offers instructions on navigating the steps. "Atta boy, Tommy, atta boy, you're doing it. Just watch yourself, don't go too fast!" The little towhead descends with agility, a testimony to his inherited athletic genes and the confidence instilled by his doting family. He stops briefly at the fishpond, watching the darting golden fish that Gamble maintains all year round. Then, scampering onto the lawn where he's dwarfed by the towering oaks, Tommy considers what to do next.

Joan agrees, paraphrasing a favorite song of hers: "A child is a child for just a moment. Hold on to that moment, you'll never see it again." That's why she so strongly supported her husband when he acted on his epiphany.

"Two or three days later, I walked into the commissioner's office and told him that I wanted to quit," Gamble says. "He asked me if I'd consider working three days a week, but I didn't even have to think about it. 'No,' I said, 'I'm done.'"

So these days, instead of Astroturf, Gamble, 66, contends with the real green stuff; and instead of running for commuter trains, he runs a G-scale outdoor train set that chugs through his fantasyland backyard.

"Let's feed the birds, Tommy," Gamble suggests, ambling over to one of several birdfeeders suspended from the overhanging branches. "We installed these pulleys so that Tommy can put in the seed himself," Gamble says as he lowers a feeder to the ground. He helps the 2-year-old pour in the seed, explaining how hungry the birds will get in the coming winter. "We keep a list up in the kitchen of all the birds that come and feed," says Gamble. "I think we're up to 40 by now."

Birds fed, Tommy's short attention span is diverted by a shrill sound coming from the grass. He and his grandmother investigate and find the noisemaker—a cicada nestled in the blades. But so are acorns, and Tommy is soon on a mission to collect them all. When his tiny hands are filled, he scatters them and starts all over. Gamble, relaxed and approving, watches from the sidelines.

"I never took a vacation in all the time that I was coaching," says Gamble, who began his outstanding career in 1954 as football coach for Clayton High School, "the smallest high school in New Jersey." Later, while coaching at Audubon High, Gamble led his team to a state championship. "Coaches get too much criticism, and too much credit," he says. "It just so happened that we had great players on that team." In 1967, Harry was named head football coach at Lafayette College, and four years later moved on to a decade as head coach at the University of Pennsylvania. From there it was the pro leagues and, ultimately, the top job with the Eagles. "I gave up golf so that I could be home with the boys. I've always tried to spend whatever free time I had at home with my family."

Family is paramount to Gamble, who has such strong memories of his own childhood that remembering his maternal grandmother reduces him to tears. "We were very close," he says, giving what little explanation he can muster. "When you are, it's a gift."

That same gift is what he realized he wanted to give Tommy that fateful morning on the train. "I hope that Joan and I can pass

on to our grandson the values about family, respect for people, and love of fun that we passed on to our boys," Gamble says.

Then, in a sudden burst of energy, Tommy runs toward his grandparents. Joan picks up an ever-present football and throws it to her husband. Harry tosses it gently to his grandson. He catches it! Then Gamble tries to center him the ball, as if Tommy were a quarterback. But the toddler refuses. Standing tall, hands on his hips, the youngest Gamble asserts himself. "When I'm older!" he says, simply and emphatically. It takes a moment for the child's wisdom to sink in. Then Harry and Joan throw back their heads and roar with laughter.

Sybil Straker

Sherri Cooper

On the occasion of her 80th birthday, Sybil Straker—"Mimi" to her grandchildren—was given the following toast by her grand-daughter, 25-year-old filmmaker Sherri Cooper.

My grandmother and I have an abnormal relationship.

I thought I'd say that before I even start my toast, so as not to set you up with some different expectations, where you'd be ready for me to describe a little old lady and cookies and milk and quiet time. No.

Mimi is a spitfire, a bosom buddy. She bought me my first bra, and helped me find something that gave me, as she put it, "a little something extra" in the cleavage. She is a soul mate, a late-night phone call, my adviser about men, my partner-in-crime shopper, the one who told me to go for it and buy the $400 leather pants. She got me drunk at her dinners, taught me about chimichangas in the '70s before Mexican food was even cool, told me about the wonders of skinny-dipping, the soothing quality of a hot bubble bath. She was my proof of real love, passion, a supporter of lace underwear, sparkly jewelry, old handbags, good shoes and good food, opera, black-and-white photos. She admitted that there was sex in the 1940s (they just called it heavy necking) and yes, sex drive carries into your 70s (now is it your 80s, Mimi?).

Mimi, you are amazing, and I am so lucky, not just to love you and be loved by you, but to say I come from your stock. You are a powerhouse, a loving force, sanity, a listening ear—a listening and biased but somewhat deaf ear—comfort, good smells, and good things. Life and love.

Happy 80th—you really don't look a day over 57, and I promise we will go rollerblading in Aspen, just like you asked!

Alexander

Olexy

Jerry Orbach

*I*n his second-floor office along Manhattan's Hudson River, Jerry Orbach sits at his desk awaiting his next call to the set of *Law & Order*, the 1997 Emmy Award–winning Best Drama Series, in which Orbach portrays Detective Lennie Briscoe. In contrast to the gloomy drizzle falling outside on the Chelsea Pier, Orbach is healthfully bronzed—thanks to artful stage makeup—and appropriately official, wearing Briscoe's tan leather gun holster around his waist. "I'm probably going to be called any minute," the versatile stage, screen, and television actor says. "But let me show you this in the meanwhile."

He swivels around and picks up two black-and-white photographs from his desk. "I look like him, don't you think?" asks Orbach, proffering two pictures: the first, a handsome, chiseled-feature profile shot. "That's me, only younger," he says of the photo, probably dating back to when 21-year-old Orbach made his New York debut as Mack the Knife in *The Threepenny Opera*. "And that's my grandfather," he says, smiling, holding up the vintage picture of a proud, high-cheekboned man to whom his grandson does, indeed, bear a resemblance. "His name was Alexander Olexy," says Orbach, "and he was quite a man."

Born in Poland, Olexy was 6 feet 3 inches and 200 pounds when he was conscripted into the czar's army. "The officers would make bets about who could knock him down with one punch," says Orbach. "Naturally, he didn't like that very much, so he got out of there, and came to America around the turn of the century."

Born in the Bronx, New York, Orbach, as a 6-year-old only child, went with his mother and father to live with his maternal grandparents, Olexy and his wife, Susan, in the house his grandfather built in Wilkes-Barre, Pennsylvania. "He was a coal miner, and I used to get up every morning in the dark with him," Orbach recalls. "While my grandmother was making up his lunch pail, I'd go get a bucket of coal from the cellar for the stove in the dining room, so she could make toast for my grandfather."

For a young boy with the kind of fertile imagination that would one day take him to Broadway and Hollywood, even a humble cellar can be a magical place. "It was wonderful down there," says Orbach. "Half of it was my grandmother's root cellar. She was a wonderful figure who also came from Poland, where she'd worked in the czar's household. She made everything from scratch—pickles from cucumbers and all kinds of preserved fruits and vegetables. She used to make wonderful cherry pies from the magnificent bing cherry tree they had in the backyard. She'd always make me two, and put my name in the crust. Believe it or not, she even made her own sausages, grinding the meat and stuffing it into the casings." He smiles. "There was always kielbasa hanging in the cellar."

The other half of the cellar was devoted to his grandfather's passion for carpentry. "He had a complete workshop down there, and I would work alongside him, making wooden swords and things." The skills Olexy taught his grandson remain with him today. "While I was filming *Dirty Dancing*, for outpatient therapy when I wasn't working, I carved a cane. It took weeks to whittle. The handle is the head of a bird, and I put stones in for the eyes," Orbach says with satisfaction.

Grandson and grandfather shared other favorite pastimes, like listening to radio dramas. "He used to call me 'Tonto,' because I was his sidekick," says Orbach, who remembers, in vivid detail, accompanying his grandfather on a memorable excursion.

"I was 7, and one weekend he took me over to the mine—Nottingham, number 13 or 17. I believe it was the deepest coal mine in the United States, hard anthracite, about a mile deep. He took me down in the elevator and showed me how, if you dug one ton of coal and loaded it in the car, you got one dollar. 'If you dig sixteen tons,' he told me, 'you get sixteen dollars.' And he showed me how you'd put your initial on the car to show it's yours. And he showed me the miners' helmets with the lights on them, and the canaries they brought down to warn them of poison gas. Then we came back up, and he turned to me and said, 'Now you've seen it. And if you have to steal, if you have to beg, whatever you have to do, never go down there again!' That was his legacy to me."

Just as Orbach finishes his story, an assistant director pokes his head into the actor's office. "We're ready for you, Jerry," he says. Orbach nods and rises, ever the professional, taking just a moment to put aside his memories and return to the work at hand—portraying a veteran New York City cop. He walks down the hallway, crowded with racks of costumes, props, and fast-walking crew members wearing beepers and talking quietly into headsets. Striding past a buffet table, Orbach questions the caterer, "What's good today?"

"For you, I've got some chicken salad sandwiches," says the young man in the apron. Orbach obligingly picks one up, eats it in a couple of bites, and smiles his approval.

On the set, he greets the cast and crew with an affable grin or a quip. Things move quickly and smoothly, and after three takes the scene is completed, and Orbach is once more at leisure. "It's about as interesting as watching grass grow, isn't it?" he laughs.

But clearly, Jerry Orbach loves the work for which he's been duly acclaimed. He garnered his first Tony Award nomination for his portrayal of Sky Masterson in the City Center revival of *Guys and Dolls*, and a Tony Award for his starring role in *Promises, Promises*. A gold record hangs on his office wall ("The platinum one's at home," he adds), won for his role as Lumière, the charming, congenial candelabra in the animated film *Beauty and the Beast*. "My two young grandchildren, Sarah Kate, and Peter, got a real kick out of that," says Orbach. "They can say they know the candlestick personally! It was one of the things that enticed me to do it. The image that I'd be like Jiminy Cricket, something for my grandchildren and great-grandchildren to enjoy."

Orbach admits that his relationship with his grandchildren is different than the close, live-in one he shared with his grandfather. "The world has changed. We see them occasionally, but we really don't get to spend a lot of time with them," says the busy actor. "Scheduling and everything. But when we do see each other, Petey jumps up on me and yells, 'Grandpa, Grandpa!' They're just terrific kids. I hope that as they grow up a little, we'll get to see more of them. But they always know we're there for them!"

Just as Orbach knew that his grandfather, who died of black lung disease when Jerry was 8 years old, was always there for him. "I remember one Easter Sunday when he gave me a dollar, and I went around treating all the neighborhood kids. He didn't get angry about that, even though that one dollar equaled digging up one ton of coal. I told you, he was quite a man!"

Phyllis Cohen

Max Cohen

"Max is my best fan!" says Phyllis Cohen of her 8-year-old grandson. "When he was in first grade, he introduced me to his teacher saying, 'This is my grandmother. Her name is Phyllis. She's the best bike rider in the world!'"

Max had reason to be proud of Phyllis. In August 1996, she biked in the Race Across America, a challenge that both excited and worried Max. "I thought she might go down a steep hill and get hurt." But when she finished, he admits, "I was impressed!"

Before the race, Phyllis had qualified for the 1997 Senior Olympics, but during the cross-country relay, she experienced significant debilitating joint pain (later diagnosed as Lyme disease). Something was clearly wrong, and Phyllis had to decide whether or not to compete.

"I knew I couldn't train properly, and therefore I wouldn't win or even place," she says. "I also knew my friends, who are the best cyclists, would be up on the winner's platform and I wouldn't, and that hurt."

But Max encouraged her. "It was a once-in-a-lifetime chance," he says, confirming his grandmother's description of him as "an old soul."

"Out of a field of 18, I didn't finish higher than seventh in any race," says Phyllis.

"But it's great that you finished!" Max says with such sincerity that Phyllis grins and cries at the same time.

Reaching over to pat her grandson's arm, she remembers, "Max was at the finish line. Usually he doesn't sit on my lap, especially around other people, but that day he came over and stayed right by my side, sat in my lap, and said, 'It's just good that you did your best!'"

Max nods. "You can't win every time," he says.

"That's what I've tried to teach him," chuckles Phyllis. "So when the words came out of his mouth, I had to listen and believe them!"

Olive Hunt

Weir,

Marion Feruzzi,

Malissa Lee

alissa Lee embodies the beauty and spirit of her dissimilar, devoted grandmothers, English-born Olive Hunt Weir and Italian-bred Marion Feruzzi.

"As a child, I was at Grandma Olive's and Grandma Marion's all the time," Malissa recalls, her animated conversation resonating Marion's exuberance, her flawless posture resembling Olive's English reserve.

"Grandma Olive's house was the world's tidiest!" Malissa says. "Even the grass was orderly! We never thought of running across it! Then we'd go to Grandma Marion's, and it was like all hell broke loose. There'd be a softball game in the front yard, dogs running around, people singing, Papa Jim [Marion's late husband] setting off firecrackers in the backyard, and always something wonderful cooking on the stove."

Malissa credits both grandmothers with providing the foundation for her varied culinary repertoire, including homemade ravioli and pesto sauce as well as Yorkshire pudding and lamb stew.

If the wonderful aromas emanating from Malissa's kitchen aren't welcoming enough, add the visual delights of her exceptional oil paintings and sewing projects that enhance her home's decor. "Grandma Olive taught me to sew, and I made everything with her old machine that she gave me."

Grandma Marion honed Malissa's social skills with weekly lunches at the Bullock's Wilshire Tea Room, a former Los Angeles landmark. "The maitre d' was so fascinated with Malissa that he'd always give us a table, even when there was a line and we didn't have reservations," says Marion.

"Papa Jim said it best," she adds with emotion. "Driving home one evening after spending a day with her, he said, 'I loved that girl from the first time I saw her, and I'll love her till the day I die.'"

Olive nods in agreement, her delicate hand reaching out at the same time as Marion's, each caressing the granddaughter who is their living legacy.

Pansy Baldwin

Frank

Geraldine

Keams

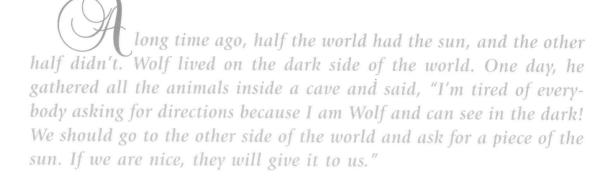

A long time ago, half the world had the sun, and the other half didn't. Wolf lived on the dark side of the world. One day, he gathered all the animals inside a cave and said, "I'm tired of everybody asking for directions because I am Wolf and can see in the dark! We should go to the other side of the world and ask for a piece of the sun. If we are nice, they will give it to us."

With her expressive voice and malleable face, Geri Keams transforms herself into Wolf, the pillar of society in an age-old Navajo creation story. At her feet a group of children sit spellbound as Geri's words stimulate their imaginations. Years ago, Geri and her eight brothers and sisters sat much the same way on the floor of their *hogan,* the traditional log-and-adobe Navajo home. There, in the Spartan environment of their Arizona reservation, they found an oasis in the stories of their grandmother, Pansy Baldwin Frank.

"When we were little, we had no running water, heat, or electricity," Geri remembers. "We had an outhouse, oil lamps, and slept on sheepskins. When it was cold, Grandma got

up throughout the night to add wood to the stove. Without radio or television, her stories were our best entertainment. We'd listen over and over to them, and when she'd finish, we'd beg her to tell them again."

Then another animal stood up. It was "Trickster," the Coyote. "No!" Coyote said. "We shouldn't be nice. We should sneak to the other side of the world and steal a piece of the sun!"

"Grandma used her stories to teach us life lessons. When we'd fight, she'd pinch our noses and say, 'Don't be like Coyote!' She still uses stories to explain things to me today. When I visit the reservation she may say, 'See that mountain? It was named after a man with a wart under his eye,' then tell me the whole story. At the end, she'll say, 'You'd think they could have named it after someone more interesting!'"

Wolf was angry at Coyote. "What do you mean we should steal a piece of the sun?" And Coyote said, "Calm down! We're not going to steal a fat piece of the sun, just a tiny piece they'll never miss."

Pansy does not know much about "the other side of the world"—the one outside the 25,000-square-mile reservation on which she has lived all her life. "As a girl, she was forced by the government to attend an Indian school," says Geri. "She and other Navajo schoolgirls were deprived of their Indian names and given flower names. So today, many of the older women are named Violet, Rose, or Lily." Pansy clings to the traditional Indian ways, speaking only Navajo and refusing to have her voice recorded or photograph taken. At 89, she believes both would sap her waning strength.

"How are we going to go to the other side of the world?" Wolf asked Coyote.

"Send me," a little voice said. From the back of the cave came a round animal with tiny ears, chubby cheeks, and a big tail. "My name is Possum and I have long, sharp claws to dig a tunnel to the other side of the world. When I get there, I'll take a piece of sun and hide it in my bushy tail."

"A tunnel! That's not a bad idea," agreed Wolf.

So Possum dug until he reached the other side of the world. But when he popped out, he was blinded by the sun.

"I cannot see!" Possum yelled. And that is why they say that today Possum only goes out at night.

Geri Keams crisscrosses the country, entertaining and educating through storytelling. She dresses in the Navajo manner, a long, colorful skirt covering her boots or skimming her handmade moccasins. Over her colorful ribbon shirt she wears silver and turquoise necklaces, one a gift to her grandmother from her late grandfather.

"I went back to the reservation and took a refresher course from my grandmother when I decided to be a storyteller," she says. "When I told her what I was going to do, she couldn't believe that I could get paid for storytelling!"

Before deciding to be a storyteller, Geri went away to college. "It was hard being away and then coming back. When I did, I was expected to help my family in so many ways that it became a real burden, and I started to stay away. My grandmother seemed to understand what I was dealing with, even though she didn't know the outside world. She'd say to me, 'Don't worry about coming home. Whenever you do, the problems will still be here.' She was my redemption."

Possum jumped at the sun, and hid a small piece in his bushy tail. But as he ran back through the tunnel, his tail got hotter and hotter.

When he ran into the cave the other animals screamed, "Possum, your tail is burning!" They threw water on it and put out the fire. Then Wolf said, "Possum, your tail is so skinny!" And, indeed, today Possum's tail looks like a rat's!

Then another voice called, "Send me!" Up to the front of the cave came a tall bird named Buzzard. "I'll go to the other side and bring back a piece of the sun on top of my beautiful crown." So Buzzard flew through the tunnel to the other side of the world. There he grabbed a piece of the sun, put it in his feathers, and flew back. But the faster he flew, the more his head burned. Flying into the cave, the other animals screamed, "Buzzard, your head is on fire!" And they threw water on his crown. Wolf looked at Buzzard and said, "Buzzard, you're bald!"

Just then a teeny, tiny voice was heard. "Send me, send me!"

"I can't see you!" said Wolf. "Come closer." From the back of the cave came the littlest creature, wending her way down on her web. It was Grandma Spider. "Grandma Spider, you can't go!" the animals cried.

"I know I'm old and slow," Grandma Spider said. "But if you give me a ball of clay, I'll go and get the sun." So the animals, having no other choice, gave Grandma Spider a ball of clay, which she made into a clay pot. Slowly she carried it through the tunnel to the other side of the world.

There, the Sun Guards, with fire bursting from their heads, were guarding the sun. But Grandma Spider was so tiny they didn't see her. She quickly took a small piece of the sun, put it in the pot, and made her way through the tunnel. The pot got heavier and heavier as she traveled, but she kept going. Finally, she reached the other side.

"Many people feel my grandmother has special powers. She's lived a hard life, taking care of the livestock, working in the cornfields, raising her own children and then all of us. Navajos traditionally don't wish for things. Instead, they live for now. But she let me go, to get the education she never had. Then she gave me what she did have, all the knowledge of her family, the Navajo mythology, my roots, my balance."

The ball of sun had gotten so big that when the other animals took the pot, the sun bounced out and landed in the sky! The animals were so happy to finally have light that they danced around Grandma Spider. And to this day, they say that if you look into the center of Grandma Spider's web, you will see the shape of the sun!

Don Bond Sr.

Ellen Bond

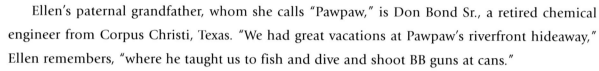hen 11th-grader Ellen Bond was assigned an oral history project, she knew immediately whom to interview. "It had to be my grandpa," the honor student says, "because I just love talking to him. He's so cool!"

Ellen's paternal grandfather, whom she calls "Pawpaw," is Don Bond Sr., a retired chemical engineer from Corpus Christi, Texas. "We had great vacations at Pawpaw's riverfront hideaway," Ellen remembers, "where he taught us to fish and dive and shoot BB guns at cans."

Before interviewing him, Ellen thought she knew her grandfather well. "He's a joker, a teaser. But when I started questioning him, I got some answers that surprised me."

Don Bond talked seriously about his experiences during World War II. "On Memorial Day," he told Ellen, "the dead are honored, but the wounded are rarely mentioned. These people deserve our greatest thanks, as they are the unending sacrifices."

"He never sounded like that before," says Ellen, who later learned from her father that Don's brother had developed epilepsy as a result of war wounds.

Another unexpected answer came when she asked Don what he'd write in a note to be read by future generations. "I'd hardly ever seen him go to church," Ellen says, "but he responded, 'Before you act, consider what Jesus would do.' I realize now that the activities he loves, especially fishing, are silent. It makes perfect sense, since I now know he's really a spiritual man."

Ellen's discoveries delight her teacher, Cynthia R. Johnson, who considers oral histories to be the most meaningful of her class projects. "Students don't usually think about their grandparents as youngsters, so they're surprised and enlightened by what they learn."

Both Ellen and Don want to continue the oral history. "It was neat to share in Ellen's assignment," says Don, "and I think it was good for Ellen to learn about a time before she was born."

"It was a very positive experience for me, too," Ellen says. "I got to really know who my grandfather is, and that changes both of us forever."

Blanche Eugenie

Newell Jewett

Celeste Holm

*H*erself the proud grandmother of three, actress Celeste Holm couldn't help but be delighted when she was named 1997's Grandparent of the Year by the National Grandparents' Day Committee. Yet, the Academy Award–winning actress protested, "The award should really go to my grandmother, Blanche Eugenie Newell Jewett!

"At a time when women didn't have many options, my grandmother became a teacher, an accomplished musician, and an orchestra conductor. I'm not afraid of anything because she wasn't afraid of anything. She held on to me, but her hands were always open," recalls Celeste.

Among her most cherished memories of her grandmother are the summers spent at the family farm, which Celeste still owns and enjoys. "Grandmother would serve lunch under the grape arbor and later, in the heat of the afternoon, she'd read *Wind in the Willows*, *The Jungle Book*, and *Winnie-the-Pooh.*"

Celeste listened carefully to her grandmother's words then, and also later, when she benefited from some prescient grandmotherly advice.

"In 1943, my grandmother was a theater critic, so I called her when I heard that Rodgers and Hammerstein were writing a new Broadway musical, *Oklahoma!* She said, 'I think this could be the most important play in the world. We're asking young men to go fight for their country, maybe even die for their country, and this play about the American West may be the most wonderful thing for people to see now.'" In her role as the raucous Ado Annie, "the girl who can't say 'no,'" Celeste Holm became a star.

Fifty years later, Celeste still believes "that the arts can bring order out of chaos." Portraying the warm, spirited grandmother, Hattie Greene, on the CBS series *Promised Land*, she brings to television what she carries forth in life. "Grandparents have so much love and a wealth of wisdom. Pass it along!"

Gloria

Jerry Lushing

Justin & Margaux

Lushing,

Brian, Joey, &

Lauren Freeman,

Andrew & Steven Dean, &

Garrett, Jeffrey, Spencer,

& Stephanie Greller

"'Are all the cousins coming?' That's always the first question the grandkids ask when they walk through the door," says Jerry Lushing, a prominent Los Angeles real estate developer, better known as "Pop Pop" to his 11 grandchildren.

"When they come here, they all just want to be together," says Lushing's comely wife, Gloria. A commercial model, community volunteer, and self-confessed frustrated actress, Gloria appears undaunted by the prospect of serving meals to 21 (herself and Jerry, four children and their spouses, and 11 grandchildren). "We use any excuse to get our children and grandchildren together. Although they live 20 minutes from us and within five minutes of each other, the kids attend different schools and don't have a chance to see each other every day. So it's important to give them an opportunity to be together. Whenever we can think of a reason to have the family over, we do so. There's no more exciting thing for the children to do than to be with their cousins."

Despite their busy work schedules and a bevy of friends who vie for their time, the Lushings rank interaction with their grandchildren as a top priority. "We get our grandchildren's school and sports schedules so we can plan to attend the events," Jerry says. "And then, of course, we make our own arrangements for activities to do with them."

"They always have exciting things for us to see and do," says granddaughter Margaux Lushing, 13. "The other night our grandparents took Lauren, me, and the three oldest boys to see the show *Cats*. We all thought it was great!" says the pretty teenager.

"They take us to see all the new museum exhibits," says 13-year-old Lauren Freeman, the firstborn grandchild. "And when Margaux and I sleep over alone, they take us to movies that the younger kids can't see." The pretty brunette also traveled to Israel and France with her grandparents over the summer. Expertly balancing her 14-month-old cousin, Garrett Greller, on her right hip, Lauren appreciatively states, "Nana and Pop Pop are more energetic than a lot of other grandparents!"

The older boys are happy beneficiaries of their grandparents' vitality. Justin Lushing, 10, enjoys golf lessons with Nana and Sunday brunches with Pop Pop at the Magic Castle, a private Hollywood club devoted to the art of illusion. Brian Freeman, 9, loves playing hide-and-seek around the garden, sailing paper airplanes from the top story of the house, and shooting hoops with his cousins. The younger children recently were treated to the stage production of *Beauty and the Beast*. "People thought we were crazy

to take a 3-year-old to a show," says Jerry. "But even the youngest sat there transfixed! I loved watching all their reactions."

"It does take a lot of thought and planning," admits Gloria, whose calendar is filled with grandkid activities.

"Sometimes I look at her day planner and wonder when we'll ever have time for our friends or ourselves," Jerry jokes.

"It is wonderful to spend time together," Gloria says. "But the things we like to do with them—the walking tours through the historical sections of Los Angeles, going to art shows, even bringing home cartons from the supermarket so the kids can make a spaceship in the backyard—don't happen by themselves. We put a lot of thought into what we do together."

Gloria concedes that losing her mother when she was a young adult might have created a gap in her life that her close, committed family now fills. The heart of this devoted family beats most strongly in the Lushings' art-filled Beverly Hills home, where neither Gloria nor Jerry has ever said to the grandchildren, "Don't touch!" But the soul of this family emanates from Gloria and Jerry's solid 35-year marriage.

"Jerry was the best man at my first wedding," says Gloria, relating the rather unorthodox way in which their romance began. "A few years later, when my marriage fell apart, I moved back to Los Angeles. By that time, Jerry's first marriage was ending, too.

We ran across each other, and you know how it feels comfortable when you meet someone from the past? Well, that's how it felt being with Jerry." It wasn't long before Gloria had a second wedding, and this time Jerry was the groom!

"I had my son, Glenn, from my first marriage, and Jerry had his children, Michael and Linda. Together, we had a daughter, Nancy. At one point, all four children lived with us together as a cohesive family," Gloria says contentedly.

"Today all our children and their spouses are good friends. They double-date, have their kids on the same Little League team, and we all go on vacations together," says Jerry, who's currently planning a holiday getaway for the whole gang.

But all this togetherness doesn't preclude having boundaries. "I would never get involved in our children's business," says Gloria. "We listen when they tell us what they're going through with the kids, but bottom line, it's their lives, and they should live them as they see fit. I may have to bite my tongue at times, but I wouldn't dream of interfering."

"We never see the things they complain about when the kids come here," says Jerry. "Maybe at times the little ones get a bit wild, but we never have to discipline them. I think that grandchildren relate differently to grandparents than they do to their parents. Maybe the parents take them a bit for granted, and vice versa. But when you're a grandparent deal-ing with your grandchildren, it's like you're dealing with jewels."

Gloria seconds her husband's sentiments. "I have everything they've ever made us—drawings, cards, letters—in boxes upstairs," she says. "I have so many love notes up there!" Suddenly, Jeffrey Greller, 10, runs by, giggling as his 6-year-old cousin, Joey Freeman, tries to catch him. Andrew and Steven Dean, 4 and 2, sit nearby busily peeling and eating oranges. A few yards away, 3-year-old Stephanie Greller enjoys the attention of her older girl cousins, and Spencer Greller, 6, wonders aloud when lunch will be ready. "It's not a rote thing," says Gloria, smiling radiantly as she observes her grandchildren. "I've got a *major* passion for each and every one of them!"

Marie Bashian

Bedikian

Written by

her granddaughter,

Leslie

Ayvazian

As a second-, third-, and fourth-grader, I went to my grandmother's house every day for lunch. We ate at her Formica table in the kitchen on the second floor of her two-family home. The third floor was the attic, where my grandfather worked in his three-piece suit at his Armenian typewriter. The first floor was a small apartment covered with pins. Nonnie had rented it to a dressmaker.

Now I live in this house, renovated by my husband, an architect, into a one-family home. I inherited the boxes, trunks, and suitcases in the basement, and the bookshelves in the attic, all filled with journals, letters, sermons (my grandfather was a minister), diaries, photographs, costumes (my grandmother was a singer), wedding clothes, silverware, silver bowls, hand-embroidered nightgowns, dressing gowns, quilts, placemats, napkins, hand towels. And hundreds of books. And hundreds of articles written by my grandfather about the Armenian people, and about God.

Living in the house, I ran my hands over everything. I read. I recalled the stories of the Old Country that were told to me as a child. Then I wrote a full-length play, which I call *Nine Armenians*. It is the story of three generations of an Armenian family living in America. The matriarch of the play is modeled after Marie Bedikian—my grandmother, Nonnie, who died at 92, her last words quietly asking the nurse, "What time is it?"

Non...I believe she tugged at my shoulder and encouraged me to write. I can see her hands touching my shirt with a "Come this way, dear" pull. I was always aware that Nonnie had unusually soft hands. She kept hand lotion on the end table next to the corner of the couch where she sat in the room that is now my dining room—the end table that held a black dial phone, a red address book, a plastic cylinder with stamps, a turquoise comb, aspirin, clear nail polish, gray bobby pins, books, letters, needle and thread to make lace, and hand lotion.

After moving to New York City, I visited Nonnie several times a month, taking the bus from the Port Authority to her tree-lined New Jersey street. She served me a meal of *tass kebob*, pilaf, *sarma*, feta cheese, and *annoushaboug*, then later, tuna salad, pilaf, and anisette cookies. Afterwards, we sat on the couch and talked. Sometimes I would put my head in her lap and she would push the hair from my face and stroke my head.

I remember Nonnie's profile, her gray, swept-up hair with the ripple in the front, which, at 49, I have discovered in my own hair. I remember her distinct, full-bodied laugh. But most often I think of her soft hands on my head and my careful feelings of pure gratitude.

Nonnie was graduated top in her class from Barnard College. She maintained her college friendships throughout her life. I watched her visit with her vivid, articulate, surprising friends: Elizabeth Sarka, who walked across Africa with her husband on her honeymoon. Elizabeth knocked on Nonnie's door one year, holding two 10-pound rocks, a gift from a quartz quarry in Vermont. Elizabeth, 84 years old, had driven from Vermont to place these rocks in the ivy by her friend's front door, now my front door. Every year, they met for lunch on Nonnie's birthday. I hosted them in my midtown loft. They sat next to each other, eyes closed, holding hands. They spoke of their gardens, politics, children, memories. Nonnie, the singer. Elizabeth, the activist. Me, the observer.

Nonnie had many vivid friends: Ruth, the author; Agavnhe, the lawyer; Olivia, her accompanist; Yvenige, her sister; and another friend, who recently touched my life through a letter I received from my mother, Nonnie's only child. She informed me that a friend of Non's, one I vaguely knew, was in possession of a box of Nonnie's letters—letters Nonnie had given her with instructions to destroy them. My mother had learned that this woman had kept them. Mom told me that Nonnie's relationship with this woman had fallen off before Non died. And Mom wanted the letters returned. So finally, after discovering the woman's unlisted phone number, we spoke. She had decided, she said, not to give me the box. The letters were hers now, she said, given to her at a time when Non had confided in her that her grandchildren were uninterested in her, perhaps didn't love her anymore...so this woman said.

I think of this lost friend and the hostage box of letters, and silently I apologize to Nonnie. I know how she felt. I know because I always knew Non's love was not unconditional. Her judgments, although never spoken, were expressed in her mouth, her eyebrows, her chin. In the face of certain issues, she became stone silent. Through my 20s, I endured several years of knit brows and held breath, as I lived in pursuit of a wonderful boyfriend. I knew she considered it more important to pursue studies, to exercise discipline, and to learn languages, literature, history. And I, rebelliously, meandered in my studies, and stayed on course in my search: Where was love? Fortunately, I found him. I married him. She loved him. And I brought him to her house, now our house. Sam and Nonnie discussed religion, architecture, cooking...and I, occasionally, would sit with my head on her knees. And she would put one hand in her lap, and with the other, gently stroke my hair.

Nonnie knew our son, Ivan, through the first 11 months of his life. At 10 months old, when he just started to walk, we immediately brought him to Non's house. Ivan spent the visit carrying the brooms from her closet to her feet. He made his way from Nonnie's corner of the couch, through the kitchen, to the broom closet. Then he returned to the couch dragging a full-size kitchen broom behind him to present to her. Non laughed and made eloquent acceptance speeches to 10-month-old Ivan. Then she kissed him and shook his hand and he wobbled off to the broom closet to collect another offering. Although Ivan has no memory of Non, he keeps a picture of their faces, nose-to-nose, on his dresser.

Now Ivan is a very tall 10-year-old. And I can see, on the rare occasions when he is not in motion, that he holds his hands in repose just as she did. Ivan's strong, artistic hands are, at rest, just as hers were when she sat with one hand on my head and the other gently in her lap.

Nonnie: a singer, a mother, a grandmother to me and my sisters, and a teacher. Nonnie, who had her mysteries. I revere her. Marie Bashian Bedikian: Guide, Inspirer, Matriarch.

Dedicated to my mother, Gloria, and my two sisters, Andrea and Gina.

The Foster Grandparent Program

Esther Coulter & Dasha Emerick

"*I* started with zero," remembers 80-year-old Esther Coulter, a volunteer "foster grandmother" from Carmichael, California. In describing the start of her tutoring relationship with then-7-year-old Dasha Emerick, Esther recalls, "Dasha was very moody. I'd never know from one day to the next if there would be tears or smiles. If I happened to touch her, she'd stiffen up and become almost catatonic. I think it probably was a reflection of the bad treatment she'd received in the orphanage," says the warmhearted woman who is one of thousands of seniors nationwide involved in the Foster Grandparent Program, a federally funded project devoted to working with children in need.

Fortunately for Dasha, "Grandma Esther" is a woman of wisdom and hands-on experience. "I began teaching in 1941 in a one-room schoolhouse in Eureka, South Dakota, where I taught nine students in seven grades. All told, I taught for 24 years, taking time out to be home with my two daughters when they were little." Later, Esther would help teach her four grandchildren to read, using games and cut-out magazine pictures for flash cards. "But each child is different," Esther says. "And you have to suit your method to that particular youngster." With Dasha, Esther eventually figured out how to combine the right amount of compassion, confidence, and control needed to reach the troubled child.

"Esther was able to reach into that little girl and bring her out," says Nancy Greenhalgh, Dasha's first-grade teacher. "At the beginning, Dasha would sit in class, unresponsive, her legs curled up under her, sucking on her fingers. But Esther came every day and worked with

her. Children really know if someone genuinely cares for them, and Esther does. Her love helped turn that girl around!"

One year after Esther's first meeting with Dasha, it's hard to imagine the bubbly, bright-eyed, active girl being any other way. As she enters the small, book-filled room that serves as the tutoring center for Garfield Elementary School, she runs over to Esther (who manages to look relatively comfortable despite having to make do with the pint-sized table and chair arrangement), and burrows her head into Esther's snow-white hair.

"Hello, little girl!" Esther greets Dasha, pulling back slightly. "I don't want to breathe on you. I have a cold and I almost stayed home."

"I don't want you staying home," Dasha says, assuming a mock pout. "I want you coming here!"

Esther laughs, gratified by the compliment, and even more by the show of self-assurance that allows Dasha to reveal her feelings. "Although I never pushed or prodded, I tried to make Dasha feel that she could talk about anything," Esther says. "But she never spoke about her past."

Dasha's roots are far from the quiet suburb of Sacramento that is now her home. Born in Siberia, where she was abandoned as an infant, she spent her critical formative years warehoused in an overcrowded, understaffed orphanage. Nancy Greenhalgh recalls that Dasha once told her that she was "born on an airplane," the one that brought her to America at the age of 4. Her adoptive mother, Julie Emerick, who also adopted a younger boy from the same orphanage, says that she never heard her daughter speak Russian. "She didn't speak at all until she was able to process everything into English. Then she began speaking spontaneously—three and four words strung together."

Dasha's physical, psychological, and cultural deprivations created a challenge for the educators who would work with her. "When she entered first grade," Esther recalls, "she was performing at a prekindergarten level. I was given 30 to 40 minutes with her every day. But for the first half of the year, a lot of that time was spent in struggle rather than learning. There were many days of trial and error. Dasha could be all smiles, but if something went wrong, if I touched her or asked her to repeat something, she'd clam up. When that happened, and she'd shut down, I'd have to take her back to her classroom and wait to see what happened the next day.

"But then, around April, I decided to try something different. Whenever she became unresponsive, I would say to her, 'Okay, if Dasha doesn't want me, I'll leave Dasha alone.' Then I'd turn my chair around, so that my back would be facing her, and I wouldn't pay attention to her until she came around.

"Do you remember those times?" Esther asks the young girl.

"Yes," mutters Dasha unhappily. "It seemed like a thousand years!"

Forgetting her cold, Esther opens her arms and gives Dasha a reassuring hug. "By the end of the year," Esther reports with obvious satisfaction, "Dasha was reading first-grade material. It took a lot of hugs, some sanctions, and more than a few tears!"

As much as Dasha has profited from time spent with her foster grandmother, Esther candidly confides that she benefits equally from volunteering. A decade ago, at an age when most wives look forward to reaping the fruits of a long-term marriage, Esther separated from her husband. "If two people are going in different directions, then you might as well live apart," she says. Newly single, Esther read about the Foster Grandparent Program in a local newspaper and soon joined the ranks of low-income seniors, 60 to 90, who work a minimum of 20 hours a week with children with special educational needs, like Dasha, as well as juvenile delinquents, substance abusers, and hospitalized, homeless, physically disabled, abused, and illiterate children.

The low hourly stipend and other small recompense the volunteers receive are clearly minor perks compared to the dramatic difference the program makes in their lives. "Without these children, I would feel empty," one foster grandmother says. "If I can't be with the kids for a day, I feel something's missing," says another.

Grandma Esther concurs. "The Foster Grandparent Program has probably kept me out of an old-age home. It's given me a sense of security, a place to go, something to do. And not just busy work, but working at what I enjoy. It has made me more outgoing and given me emotional stability."

Dasha reaches out and touches Grandma Esther's hand. When, in return, she receives a smile from her foster grandmother, she beams. "It's all about working with people," Esther Coulter says. "You have to get involved in people's lives."

Jan Kwea Lee Liu

David Liu

*S*eated at the kitchen table in his family's Northern California hillside home, David Liu wrestles with the question of his ethnicity. "I don't really know what being Chinese is," admits the 22-year-old high-tech entrepreneur. Staring out the window at the maze of rooftops and trees that run down to the bay below, he ponders the questions that have nagged him all his life: Who is he? What is he? Unlike many children given up by their unwed natural parents, David is well aware of his biological roots. But still the dilemma about his identity remains.

"My Chinese friends say that I'm not really Chinese, maybe because of the way I dress, or the way I act..." he says. Just then, the piercing whistle of a kettle prompts him to rise and prepare tea, which he brings to the table. "Here, *Nai Nai*," David says, placing the mug in front of Jan Kwea Lee Liu, his 74-year-old paternal grandmother who has devoted much of the last two decades of her life to raising her grandson. The wiry, gray-haired woman looks up at her grandson, then peers into the steaming green beverage for a moment. Nodding her approval, she takes a cautious sip, then sets the cup down next to her small, black electronic translator that converts English words into Chinese symbols.

"I'm the last Liu male," David says. "I have cousins and a half-sister, but in my immediate family, I'm the only male of my generation." Perhaps this privileged position explains the way in which the Liu family embraced David since his birth in Taiwan in 1975 and made his upbringing truly "a family affair."

"My Aunt Lifong is, by law, my mother, my legal guardian," David explains. "But because she frequently traveled for business, most of the day-to-day responsibility for raising me fell to my grandmother and grandfather."

Mrs. Liu and her husband, Chung-Chi, were raised in Hunan Province, in sight of Chairman Mao's mountaintop home. With the Communist takeover of China in the late 1940s, they fled to Taiwan, where they steadfastly retained their traditions and customs. These they tried to impart to David, who does his best to translate his grandmother's thoughts on her aspirations for him.

"I often taught David those principles of how to be a decent person," Mrs. Liu says in her native Mandarin dialect, her voice filled with conviction. "I wanted him to know how to handle things properly, hoping that when he grew up he could be a useful person."

When David was 5, his Aunt Lifong decided to move the family to San Francisco, where she believed David would enjoy greater opportunities. Although unschooled in English and American customs, David rapidly adjusted to his new and challenging environment. "I got picked on at first, because I was so different," he recalls. "I didn't know how to ask for anything I wanted, so I got taken advantage of a lot. Some kids were really pretty nasty. My aunt insisted that I speak English at home, and her younger sister and I watched cartoons on TV, over and over, and that's how I learned English." Soon, young David was speaking English exclusively, and, for the first time in his life, a barrier developed between him and his traditional grandmother, who was more comfortable preserving her past and remaining unassimilated.

"My grandmother wore long, mandarin-collared clothing," David remembers, "while my friends' mothers wore tennis clothes and drove carpool." As David grew older and more prone to peer pressure, his grandmother's provincial ways became an embarrassment. Yearning for acceptance, he pulled away from the traditions that had been the cornerstone of his young life. "I was developing in the way of the non-Chinese," David says, "and soon I made no efforts to continue with the Chinese way of being." Once closer to him than anyone else in the world, his grandmother was now on the periphery of her grandson's life.

"By the time I was 14, I was a spoiled punk," David admits. "Strictly an MTV kid, taking for granted all that we have here— music, stereos, television." So it was very begrudgingly that David accompanied his aunt, her husband, Joseph, and his grandmother on a trip back to mainland China, where Jan Kwea Lee Liu was to be reunited with her sister for the first time in 40 years.

Only in hindsight can David fully understand why he was so sullen and uncooperative during the trip. "Although I had successfully integrated into American life, it had been very difficult initially. I knew that I looked different from everyone else here, and I didn't want to go to China and be reminded that I was like them and not like my American friends."

Translating for his grandmother, he relates her own apprehensions about traveling to the remote third-world village of her youth. "I was quite worried that my daughter, her husband, and my grandson would not be used to the living conditions and that they could not adjust, especially in the country where the hygienic conditions and the water are so bad." Wisely, however, Mrs. Liu knew that David would benefit from the experience. "I wanted him to see where both sides of his family came from, our birth-places and the families' burial grounds." Believing David to be "an honest, responsible, and diligent boy," somewhere in her heart Jan Kwea Lee Liu harbored the hope that more than one reunion would take place on their journey.

After an initial stop in Hong Kong and an arduous trek into the provinces, the emotional family reunion finally took place in his grandmother's old village. "I wore jeans and my San Francisco Giants baseball cap pulled down over my eyes," says David, who remembers standing on the sidelines, refusing to be included in the celebration.

On the second day, however, there was a turning point. "It was Joseph, Lifong's husband, the man I consider to be my father, who brought it about," says David. "He took me aside and told me that I was acting like a real jerk, being rude, ignoring my rela-tives who were trying so hard to be nice to me." The admonition hit David like a thunderbolt. Suddenly, he began to see his grandmother's family—*his family*—with new eyes. "I realized I'd prejudged everyone, thinking they were nobodies, so behind the times because they didn't have the things that I had back home."

Gradually, the young teenager extended himself—first to an uncle who gave him a trinket carved from bamboo; then to another who offered a puzzle woven from string. A relative who looked like JFK made David laugh despite their language barrier; another impressed him by carrying heavy water buckets sus-pended from a pole across his strong back.

By the end of the third day, David took off his baseball cap as a sign of respect for his family, who prevail with dignity and courage despite the diffi-culties they face.

"It was also then that I realized how my grandmother had loved and spoiled me with her time and atten-tion throughout my life. It took the China trip to show me what she had given me all of those years."

For Mrs. Liu, her hopes had been realized. Not only had she been reunited with her sister and her past, but she had also been reconciled with her grandson, who was her present and her future. "Coming back from China," she says, "I found that David was much more mature and respectful." Modestly, as is her way, she takes no credit for his transformation but does express her pride. "With this kind of grandson we all feel very content."

Mae White,

Carol Burnett,

Zachary Carlson

Carol Burnett's youngest daughter was about to give birth, and the famous grandma-to-be decided that this was one time she should stay out of the spotlight. "I didn't want to intrude on Erin and my son-in-law, so I didn't go into the birthing room, but I did peek through a curtain. Erin was working so hard! I was so proud of what she was doing, how hard she was working, that every time she pushed, I pushed, too! We were both so worn out by the time the baby came, I don't think there was a push left in either of us!" And what did this legendary star feel when, instead of the usual applause for her efforts, she heard Zachary Carlson's first cry? "It just blew me away! The thought of my baby *having* a baby, I just broke down and wept."

Little Zach has a lot to look forward to. "It's Auntie Mame time!" Carol laughs, anticipating the hours she'll spend with her grandson watching tapes of her classic variety show. "The poor kid doesn't have a chance! Can you imagine all the *shtick* he'll pick up from Harvey and Tim!" Ensuring that Zachary develops his sense of humor is one of the two wishes Carol has for him. The other is that he have the belief that he can do anything he sets his mind to. "I got that from Nanny," Carol says. "I could do no wrong in her eyes. She gave me a feeling of confidence. For her, I was the best in the world!"

Nanny, Mae White, was Carol's maternal grandmother, who became the center of Carol's life when her parents left San Antonio to try to make it in California. Despite

Nanny being constantly worried about money, Carol recalls those days with her and her great-grandmother, Goggy, as happy ones. "We'd sit on the porch at sundown and shell peas. I loved the sound of them falling into the metal pot. Goggy would hum a religious song under her breath, and Nanny would go on and on about her father, 'the finest man who ever lived.' Goggy, however, never said a word about him."

At one point, Carol was shipped out West to join her parents. But her father, Jody, whom she adored, was an alcoholic who couldn't hold down a job. When her parents separated, Carol was sent back to Texas, and once again she was placed under Nanny's vigilant protection. "When we would go downtown, she'd hold my hand in a grip like a vise, so there was no way I could get lost," Carol remembers. While this might have been confining for another child, to Carol it was a reassuring sign of her grandmother's love and devotion.

Eventually, Louise Burnett, Carol's Joan Crawford–look-alike mother, sent for her daughter and mother to join her in California. She brought them to the building where she lived, in the shadow of the mountains bearing the HOLLYWOODLAND sign. "We were one block north of Hollywood Boulevard, but we could have been a million miles away for all that meant," says Carol.

Louise, who now had a drinking problem of her own and was continually frustrated by her inability to realize her dream of being a celebrity columnist, moved Nanny and Carol into Room 102, just down the hall from her own room. "Nanny never doubted for a minute that she and I would live together." Since Nanny was the only

"parent" whom Carol had ever lived with for any length of time, it wasn't surprising that Carol had developed a dread of losing her. This fear was exacerbated by her grandmother's nocturnal "attacks," when she'd collapse onto her Murphy bed, monitor her racing pulse, and wail, "I'm having a hissy fit, I'm going… I'm going." Carol became fearful of leaving the apartment and going to school, afraid that Nanny might die while she was gone. Because Nanny insisted she go to avoid their being arrested, Carol claims to have willed herself to get the measles so she could stay home with Nanny for a whole month.

Their mutual dependence produced an obsessive going-off-to-school ritual. "I'd kiss her good-bye, then leave the apartment, cross the lobby, open the door, turn around, and she'd be there waving, only about 7 feet away. Then I'd wave back, blow her a kiss, and go through the lobby door. I'd look back, and she'd blow a kiss back to me. Then when I was outside, I'd look back again, and she'd be at the lobby door, and we'd kiss-kiss, blow-blow, and then halfway down the street, I'd turn and see her little head peeking around the corner of the building."

Later, when Carol went off to UCLA and discovered her passion for acting, she finally began to separate from Nanny. By this time, she was able to differentiate between Nanny's fits of hypochondria and real bouts with illness. "I started to realize that there were times when Nanny would claim to be having 'an attack' and make me think she was dying. But then, someone would come by and say, 'Let's go to the picture show,' and all of a sudden, Nanny would jump up and be just fine!"

50

Carol's new-found sense of independence and her dreams of becoming an actress didn't please Nanny. "When I graduated and went off to New York, she sent me very discouraging letters that made me feel so sad. 'If you're so good, how come you don't have a job already?' she'd write. But she always pawned that kind of stuff off on my mother, saying those were her thoughts. But I knew they were Nanny's."

Carol continued to write back dutifully. "It was like keeping a diary. I did it even when there was nothing interesting to say: 'This morning I got up and had breakfast with the girls, then I went out to try and get an agent.' I wrote every day because if she didn't get a letter *each* day, even if it was the mail's fault and she got two the next, I'd hear about it! Those letters from her really bothered me. Sometimes I'd get so upset that I'd cry!"

But with all the guilt-provoking machinations and crazy-making lifestyle, being with Nanny could be fun, too, and those are the kinds of memories that Carol will, no doubt, share with her grandson. Like the scams Nanny pulled on the WPA social worker, so that there would always be enough money sewed into the sock kept under the Murphy bed to splurge on their favorite outing. "We'd go to the movies, then afterwards to Thrifty's for a vanilla ice cream soda. We both loved musicals, and Nanny particularly liked romance pictures. However, we both

really disliked *Citizen Kane*. I was too young to appreciate it, and Nanny was bored to death. Of course, once she paid for the tickets, she wouldn't leave until the movie was over, so we sat through the whole picture. When we were getting ready to hightail it out of the theater, all of a sudden there was a blackout—this was during the war—and we had to stay and sit through the whole movie a second time."

Did Carol think being raised by her grandmother was abnormal?

"What do you know when you're a kid? My best friend, Ilomay Sills, also lived with her grandmother. It wasn't that I wished I was with Mama and Daddy. When you're a kid, whatever way you're being treated seems like the norm. For me, Nanny was always *it*," Carol remembers. "As crazy and eccentric as she was, she was a mother lion. I don't know how Chrissy and I would have ever survived without her."

Chrissy is Carol's half-sister, over whom Carol quickly assumed the role of protector, despite Nanny's always trying to make everything right for the girls. "She managed to give us the little stability we had," Carol says. "We always knew she loved us." Just as Nanny knew that Carol loved her when, each week, at the close of her award-winning comedy show, she'd give that little tug on her ear, sending a secret signal to her grandmother, the woman who raised her. Just as Zachary will know the love of *his* grandmother, who has the heart and spirit to appreciate love in its many forms.

Joseph

Christian Eicher

Samuel Hartman

"People don't sing at parties anymore," Sam Hartman says regretfully, remembering the large family gatherings of his childhood. "My father had Caruso records this thick," he indicates with his fingers, "and Sousa marches that my brother, Fred, and I would parade around the house to, until the Victrola ran down and we'd have to run back to the parlor and wind it up again."

In Sam's household, the most anticipated vocal event of the year occurred on New Year's Eve, when Hartman's maternal grandfather, Joseph Christian Eicher, would perform his specialty for the family. "At midnight, Grandpa would call us all together. Then, when we were as quiet as we could be, he would begin to yodel. We'd talk about it for days after. It set us apart. Who else had a grandfather who came over from Switzerland and could yodel?"

At age 82, with a full head of hair that men half his age would envy, Hartman has wonderful recall of his youthful days. Over the last two years, his vivid memories have served as a rich resource since discovering a new avocation—writing. To combat loneliness after his second wife, Hazel, died, Hartman joined a seniors' writing workshop. Now, every Friday afternoon, he joins a dozen men and women—mostly octogenarians—to share their rich biographical remembrances. Many of Hartman's are about his grandfather, whom he acknowledges as being "closer to me than my own father."

Joseph Eicher and his grandson, whose name, when pronounced with a thick Swiss-German accent, came out "Sam-ool," lived only blocks from each other in rural New Jersey. On Sunday mornings they'd walk up into the cow pasture, where Eicher would pick mushrooms that the family would enjoy later at dinner. There were also pinochle games—in which Sam swears, "Nobody could beat Grandpa!"—and frequent fishing outings. Eicher, an avid fisherman, believed, "You can always remember the days you go fishing, but you can never remember the days you work."

"Grandpa smoked the vilest-smelling cigars in the world," Sam laughs. "When he was fishing, if the cigar went up in his mouth, it meant he had a bite. Since Grandpa didn't talk much, you had better know that also meant to slow the boat down and be ready for his next signal. A subsequent nod toward the bottom of the boat meant 'Get the net!' Now came the heart-stopping part. If you failed to net the fish, that was a sin beyond pardon. Grandpa would turn purple. You were doomed!"

Like Hartman's today, Eicher's hair was white. He wore a mustache and, although not a big man in stature, seemed to his grandson "to be a giant." When he was in his 50s, Eicher suffered a heart attack and was warned by his doctor to get his affairs in order as he hadn't much time left. But Eicher carried on despite the gloomy prognosis and managed to outlive the miscalculating physician by 20 years. "Every time Grandpa celebrated a birthday, he'd always raise his wine glass and make a toast to the long-departed doctor," Hartman chuckles. The wine glass, by the way, was filled with wine made by Eicher, an art learned during his days as a wine and cheese maker in a Swiss castle.

His grandfather's philosophy of "seeing life as it is, handling whatever comes your way" has stood Hartman in good stead. He watched his grandfather accumulate a fortune after inventing a steel-tension spring that outlasted the porcelain ones used on silk looms in the local factories. After convincing his boss that his spring would save thousands of hours in downtime, Eicher went on to patent the invention and start his own company. "We all worked to produce the springs, sitting at home in a makeshift assembly line," Sam says. "My job was to measure and cut pieces of wire. When there were 100 pieces, they were wrapped in a bundle and Grandpa took over from there."

Eicher went on to invest his profits in copper mines, and then lost everything during the stock market crash of 1929. "I remember him calling everyone in the family together and saying, 'Well, I had nothing when I came to America, and I have nothing now. I guess I'll just have to start over.'"

Subliminally, at least, Hartman must have recalled those words when, years later, he faced his own most difficult life challenge—losing his first wife, Beryl, and being left alone with two small sons. "Looking back, it seems to be a terrible nightmare," Hartman says. "I lived through it, but I don't know how I managed." Although he was in such serious debt from hospital and doctor bills that friends advised him to declare bankruptcy, Sam steadfastly refused. He worked 10-hour days, six days a week, food shopping, cooking dinner, doing laundry, helping with homework, and, of course, "cleaning up snotty noses." He dropped 60 pounds and looked like "a bag of bones" when he met Hazel one year later. "I told her she must be really hard-up if she wanted me!" Sam jokes. Today, he reveres his second wife's memory, showing off her intricate needlepoint pillows and wall hangings. Much of his former activity is curtailed because "there's no one to do it with."

But one of the things Sam has done alone is a labor of love that he started more than half a century ago. When his first son turned 1 year old, Sam began compiling his family tree. He remembers the inspiration coming to him on the day he brought his newborn son to see his grandfather, who was near death. "He recognized that this baby was his great-grandchild," Sam says. "Four days later, he passed away." Using annotations in family Bibles dating back to 1780 and information on scraps of paper, folded and unfolded so many times that he feared they would disintegrate while he read them, Hartman began to create a legacy for future generations. Today, after conquering a computer software program that helped him polish and perfect his project, Sam proudly displays the finished volume, which he's presented to his three sons and five grandchildren. On the front page is an anonymous quote: "To forget one's ancestors is to be a branch without a source, a tree without a root."

Sam Hartman has insured that his progeny are securely rooted, that they know of and about their ancestors. And through his research and rumination, he has also concluded that he was right as a youngster when he thought he would grow up and be just like his grandpa. "Truer words were never spoken," Hartman wrote. "Now that I am a grandpa, I've finally concluded that my grandpa was shrewd and, like me, partially deaf. Most times when there is background noise, I can't sort out what is being said, and like Grandpa before me, wish that I were somewhere else. I pretend I'm aware of what's going on around me and occasionally nod my head and smile. I learned that from Grandpa, but *it works*! So why argue with success?"

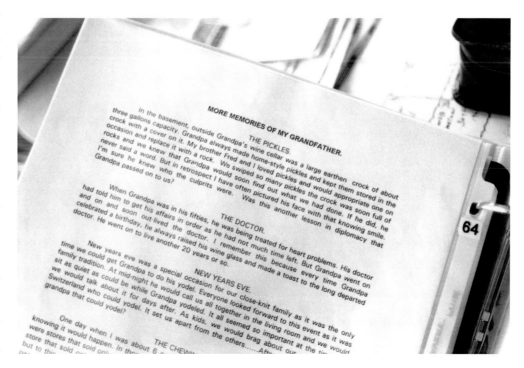

Harold

Ruth Glass

Jordan Katz

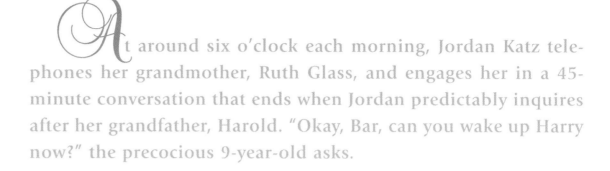

At around six o'clock each morning, Jordan Katz telephones her grandmother, Ruth Glass, and engages her in a 45-minute conversation that ends when Jordan predictably inquires after her grandfather, Harold. "Okay, Bar, can you wake up Harry now?" the precocious 9-year-old asks.

Perhaps the only unoriginal aspect of the relationship that this inventive trio shares are the names that Jordan has appropriated for them—Bar and Harry—given to Ruth and Harold years ago by one of their two older grandchildren. "When my cousin Danny was little he tried to say, 'Ma,' but it came out, 'Ba,'" Jordan explains. "I just changed it a bit to 'Bar.'"

When Harold, a former high school English and history teacher in his native Johannesburg, comes on the line, the sunrise call moves into a new dimension. "At first, Harry gets on the phone and usually gives me the news," Jordan says. "But Bar's pretty much covered that already."

"And then you play your special game, don't you?" inquires Ruth, an attractive, petite brunette whose charming manner is enhanced by her engaging South African accent. "I'm not

privy to their game," she quickly adds. "But I know they've been playing it for years."

"Since I was 4!" says Jordan, whose obvious enthusiasm implies that "the game" is a highlight of her conversations with Harold. Although she declines to reveal the exact nature of the fictitious world she and her grandfather have fabricated, she's willing to provide the tiniest tease. "Our game's a secret," she says proprietarily. "I really prefer not to share it, but I will say that we still have some of the same characters we had when we first started playing years ago."

"Jordan directs the game totally," says Harold. A serious and talented, but as yet unpublished, writer himself, he demonstrates the highest respect for his granddaughter's creations. "Jordan adds characters to our game every few weeks. It's like a soap opera. Some die, some go away..."

"And then the next week they just come back," says Jordan mischievously.

In her grandparents' apartment, which is located only a short jog from the Pacific Ocean, Jordan is encouraged to explore and expand her creative horizons. A desktop computer set up in the living room stores her writing and poetry. Harold has promised her that when she has a sizable enough collection, he will self-publish her work. "I try to write," he says. "Jordan's mother, Linzi, is a good writer. I suppose there's an urge in me to try and make one of my offspring a successful writer. I want somebody to get a good book published!"

Jordan's also a natural artist. Her colorful, eye-catching drawings and portraits are reminders of Picasso's statement that it took him a lifetime to learn to paint like a child.

"I made this in class," Jordan says, bringing over a black-faced crepe-paper doll that Ruth displays on an end table. "It wasn't an assignment. It was just something I wanted to make," she says. "It's my African doll."

"Jordi, do you remember the trip we all took to South Africa?" Ruth asks.

"I remember seeing a giraffe next to the freeway," Jordan recollects, despite having been only 3 years old when she made the long journey.

"That was when we were on safari in Kruger National Park," says Harold. "Do you remember the monkeys playing on top of the car?"

"I think I do," says Jordan. "But what I really remember is when a monkey came and started playing with the *Wizard of Oz* dolls I used to have. I mean I still have them," she says. "I just don't play with them anymore. Anyway, it was kind of fun."

Having immigrated to the United States in 1978, Harold and Ruth were eager to treat their daughters to a trip back home, accompanied by their husbands and children. "There were 14 of us," says Ruth, adding with a discernible shudder, "and 30 pieces of luggage! Even though Jordan was so young, I think that she does remember a lot, and I know that she certainly has feelings for South Africa."

"Definitely," Jordan agrees. "When people ask me what I am, I always say I'm half–South African, and I'm very, very proud of that. One of the reasons I like it so much is that it's unusual. There aren't many kids who can say that they're part South African. Oh, I'm part Canadian, too," she makes a point of adding. "From my other grandfather!"

Ruth and Harold plan to take their granddaughter back to South Africa when she's older. "I know it will mean a lot more to me then," the young girl acknowledges. Meanwhile, she loves hearing childhood stories about her grandparents and their children, and the life they lived so many thousands of miles away.

"Tell the one about your appendix, Bar!" Jordan urges. "That's my favorite!"

"Oh, Jordi!" Ruth shakes her head. "That's a terrible story!"

"But it got you out of the test!" says Jordan.

"Yes, it did," Ruth laughs. "It happened when I was 14.

One day, my Latin teacher put a test on the board and I just knew I couldn't do it. So I jumped up, grabbed my stomach, and ran out of the classroom. The teacher ran after me to find out what was the matter, and I told her I had this terrible stomachache. When they rushed me to the hospital, it turned out that I had to have my appendix taken out immediately! The teacher was so concerned that she sent me a bouquet of flowers!"

Jordan laughs and offers a ready explanation for her enjoyment of the story she's heard repeated so many times. "I've done things that I shouldn't have done, and when I find out that Harry or Bar, or my mother, or my aunts did bad things, too, I don't feel quite as guilty about what I've done."

Stories, childhood and otherwise, abound in this creative household. When Jordan was 4, Harold began to read Shakespeare to her, as well as Greek mythology, which remains one of Jordan's favorite subjects. "I like that they're not fairy tales," she says. "And they don't always have a happy ending."

Today, while Jordan's parents are going through a divorce, her grandparents' home is more than ever a haven of companionship and support.

"I think there is a difference about coming over here now," Jordan admits. "Because now when I come here, I have more things on my mind that I can discuss with Bar and Harry."

"Harold and I were considering what our role is at this time in Jordan's life," Ruth says.

"The way we saw it," Harold explains, "is that Jordan is like a little ship, a boat going off on life's journey. Her parents are her anchors; they're both lovely people whom we love deeply. All life is about going through little bumps and storms, and at the moment, Jordan's going through a kind of emotional storm. We think we're the lighthouse. When she's drifting a little far from shore, and the sea's getting rough, she sees our light and it gives her the feeling that it's going to be okay. That's how we feel about it. Do you get that feeling, Jordan?"

"Yes," she says, patting her grandmother's hand, which rests lovingly on her arm.

President

Dwight D.

Eisenhower

David

Eisenhower

wight D. Eisenhower, Supreme Commander of the Allied Forces in the European Theater of Operations during World War II and 34th President of the United States, once hired his namesake grandson, David Eisenhower, to perform the un-presidential task of painting a barn. Not surprisingly, the young boy allowed himself to get sidetracked from his task, and spent one full afternoon playing cards with a friend. When his grand-father discovered that his grandson was AWOL from his appointed post, David remembers the unhappy result: looking into what he termed his grandfather's "Bessemer furnace temper." Ike spoke only two words to his errant grandson: "You're fired!"

Although his grandfather later forgave him, David remembers the disciplined man as "dynamic, forbidding, judgmental, and intense." Nevertheless, he admits to holding him in reverence, and has devoted a good part of his adult life to researching and writing about the older Eisenhower's distinguished military and political careers.

David Eisenhower II broke rank with his family by joining the Navy instead of the Army and going to law school instead of embarking on a military career. But, like his grandfather, he is described as modest, intelligent, and likable. And, also like his grandfather, he even-tually turned to writing, something that Ike did prodigiously.

"I confess that I knew very little about my grandfather before I started this book," David said when discussing his critically acclaimed *Eisenhower: At War, 1943-1945*, which was published in 1986. "What's enabled me to spend 12 years on this book," he explained, "is my affection for my grandfather, and the personal stake that all of us in the family have in how he's perceived."

Reviewers praised David for his dispassionate presentation of his grandfather's positions, one stating, "This [book] is more than an act of piety. It is a contribution to historical understanding." It is also obviously a tribute, from a grandson to a grandfather. Perhaps, in some way, it's also an acknowledgment by David of an earlier honor bestowed on him by his grandfather.

Nestled in the woods of Maryland is a 5,500-acre park constructed by WPA workers in the late 1930s, and first used as a secret presidential retreat by President Franklin D. Roosevelt in 1942. With security insured by Marine patrols, the camp, then known as Shangri-La, was utilized frequently during World War II for conferences on war strategy. Winston Churchill and Anthony Eden were guests on numerous occasions.

Although President Truman did not care for the camp, and made little use of it, President Eisenhower visited frequently. Shortly after his inauguration in 1953, Ike changed the name to Camp David, after his only grandson.

Camp David has become part of the contemporary vocabulary. In 1959, Eisenhower hosted Nikita Khrushchev at the rustic hideaway, and the resulting improvement in attitude between the world leaders became known as "the spirit of Camp David." In September 1978, President Jimmy Carter conducted Middle East peace negotiations at the retreat between Egyptian President Anwar Sadat and Israeli Prime Minister Menachem Begin, which evolved into the precedent-setting Camp David Accord.

In words and deeds, grandfather and grandson paid each other a lasting tribute that confirmed their mutual affection, admiration, and love.

Jeannie
Epper

Christopher
Epper

Every grandson thinks his grandmother is special, but 12-year-old Christopher Epper has good reason to do so. "She's the only grandma I know of who jumps off buildings," the blond boy says earnestly.

Jumping off buildings, crashing cars, racing motorcycles, surviving avalanches, and being set on fire are what Chris' grandmother, Jeannie Epper, does for a living. Since starting in the business at age 9, she has doubled for some of Hollywood's most recognizable faces, including Shirley MacLaine, Cybill Shepherd, and Kathleen Turner. Doubling for Turner in the blockbuster film *Romancing the Stone*, Jeannie won the Most Spectacular Stunt Sequence Award in 1985. Now, over a decade later, Epper (who looks a couple of decades younger than her years) has recently completed work in the stunt spectacles *The Rock*, *Independence Day*, and *Con Air*. As president of the Stuntwomen's Association of Motion Pictures, Inc., she is involved in every phase of stunt work, a legacy from her father, and one that she passes on to succeeding generations of her family.

"I did my first movie stunt when I was 5," Chris says, his left ankle, recently broken in an ill-fated motorcycle jump, propped up on the coffee table. "I don't remember that first stunt real well, except that I had to stand on the outside of a car..."

"It was the running board of a Volkswagen," Jeannie says, always vigilant about stunt details.

"Right, and I had to hold on to a handle inside the door while the car raced down a canyon road. It was a lot of fun."

It was the same kind of fun enjoyed by Jeannie Epper and her five siblings growing up in North Hollywood, riding horses every day and coming back home only when they were hungry. "It was a different world then," Jeannie says. "You didn't have to worry about where your kids were, or what they were doing." Well, maybe you did—if the kids were the Eppers!

"After school we'd mess around, jumping out of trees onto our horses, or jumping off a horse onto a slow-moving train," Jeannie recalls. "I thank my parents daily for allowing us to do the things we did and to become the people we are today."

Those people (except for sister Margo, who quit the movie business to become a horse trainer) are all respected figures in stunt work, the field in which Jeannie's father, Johnny, made his name and set the course for his family.

"My father was from a wealthy and strict Swiss family that expected him to become an architect. But he was a bit on the wild side," Jeannie chuckles, "and joined the Swiss cavalry instead. In 1925, he visited America, and never went back home. He made his way to California and opened a riding academy in Burbank, where he met a lot of famous people, including Erroll Flynn and Gary Cooper.

"One day, he had to deliver a horse to a movie set; but when he got there, the actor, who was playing a cowboy, couldn't get the horse to jump over a car. The horse just *wasn't* going to do it! So the director asked my father if he could do it, and my father said, 'No problem.' When he told the story later, he always said he just *knew* he could do it. One take," Jeannie says proudly, "and Johnny Epper was in the movie business!"

If she sounds cavalier about how one gets into stunt work, Jeannie is anything but, especially when it comes to Chris. "We're really cautious about how he's being trained. My oldest son, Richard, is basically the one who's training him. We always talk out a stunt first and, if Christopher has any questions, he'll ask me, his uncles, or his mom, Eurlyne, who's also a stuntwoman."

Chris illustrates the family's prowess by displaying a heart-stopping photograph of his uncle Richard soaring over water, executing a motorcycle jump off a dock and into a cluttered Chinese junk. "This was for a Jackie Chan movie," Chris says. "If he didn't get the jump just right, he'd have smashed into the other dock."

Jeannie eyes the photograph and admits that she's glad she didn't know about the stunt before her son did it. "I got a call the next day from Hong Kong, and one of the other stuntmen told me that everything had gone okay. I said, 'Okay with what?' Then he told me about Richard's jump. If I'd known, I wouldn't have slept all night."

When doing her own work, Jeannie relies on her considerable experience, her fellow workers, and a lot of visualization. "You imagine yourself doing the stunt and getting through it properly." But some stunts defy good intentions and planning. "When I did the mud slide in *Romancing the Stone*, my body hit the bottom before my mind did," Jeannie remembers. "The stunts that are most frightening for me are the ones involving natural forces that you can't control."

Another thing Jeannie knows you can't control is longevity in the film business. "Even in my prime, when I was working constantly, it was difficult. Stuntpeople may not have to go through the same 'beauty thing' that actresses do, but we have to keep ourselves physically fit. You have to go to the gym. You can't go to parties if you're turning a car over the next morning. Your life, and the lives of other people, depend on what you do, so it takes a lot of discipline, and some people just don't have it."

Jeannie was the first child to do movie stunt work. "They used to use Little People to double for child actors," she says, "but they never really looked like children close-up. So, one day, my father asked if I wanted to go to work with him and ride a horse down a hill, and that's how it started. It could have been any of us kids, but I just happened to be the right size."

What is it like to be a kid doing stunts in the movies? Chris says, "It's pretty normal. When I tell my friends that I jumped off a building into an airbag, they go, 'That's pretty cool. I want to do that!' Basically, I like trying stuff I haven't done before. So do my friends. So I guess I'm just like any average kid," he says modestly.

His grandmother would dispute that. "One of the things I'm proudest of about Chris," Jeannie says, "is how well he gets along with people." She's especially proud of their joint volunteering at the Motion Picture and Television Fund Home.

"The first time we went there, I could see that it was difficult for Chris. Some of the residents have Alzheimer's and they'd reach out for him, crying and shouting. But, by the third time we visited, Chris was the way he is on the movie set, talking to everybody, making friends, and getting people to feel comfortable around him."

Another time that Jeannie remembers fondly is when Chris' sixth-grade class celebrated Grandparents' Day. "And she was the only grandma swinging upside down from the jungle gym," Chris laughs. "My friends all think she's so cool. They always ask if they can come over to Jeannie's house."

"You know," Jeannie muses, "you never call me Grandma."

"No, sometimes I call you G.G., but mostly, I just call you Jeannie."

"Do you remember when you were really little?" Jeannie asks, rubbing Chris' arm. "I took you to the set where I was working, and when I came out of the trailer you yelled, 'There's my Jeannie Epper!'"

Chris shakes his head. It's a memory too far back to be recalled. Then he glances over at the photo of his uncle Richard, soaring through the Hong Kong sky, about to nail a spectacular stunt, and an Epper smile breaks out across his face. Like his grandmother has taught him, he's imagining the stunt and how he'd get through it.

A Thousand Words About

Kim

By her grandmother,

Jean Craig

I waited breathlessly for Kim. Not only was she the first grandchild—a new generation leaving an inky footprint—but she was due a few months after the death from cancer of my husband, Ed, and thus a reaffirmation of life. She was two weeks late, which put an even sharper edge on the anticipation, and I was stunned the first time I saw her. She was so like her mother, my middle daughter, Erin, I was swept backward and stumbled about in a daze of memories. The comfort and security of life replicating itself was salve on my grief.

Kimmy ate and slept and nursed and learned to smile. At 6 months, she had reached her arms to be picked up out of the crib. She was teething, eating solid food, laughing at silly grown-up faces. I did notice she couldn't always hold her head up and it skewed to one side. "She's tippy-headed," I remarked to Erin. It was nothing, but I felt a strange jolt.

Kimmy crawled late—at 14 months. But the pediatrician said, "Babies each have their own clock. It doesn't mean anything." I found her an enormously bright child. There were stairs in my two-story home, and as protection I taught her, in two minutes, to scoot down on her fanny. I have a picture of her at 16 months pointing to her mother among a collection of family photos in my living room.

But at 20 months, she still wasn't walking and her head still tipped. Sensitized to illness by the untimely deaths of two husbands, the hair raised on the back of my neck. Around that time, Erin noticed Kim wasn't using the words she'd acquired. Bird. Dog. Mama. She hadn't said them in days or weeks. In fact, she'd quit the typical toddler babbling. Alarm set in.

Erin and Rich began an exhaustive search for answers. She wasn't walking. She'd had language and lost it, and there were new signs. Occasionally, she'd drift away mentally—"zone out," as Erin put it. Specialist after specialist after specialist couldn't find anything. Her legs were fine. Her senses were intact. But I took her to the beach when she came to visit and watched in fear as she poured sand endlessly into a bucket. She would have sat and poured it without interruption all day.

"Please, God, don't let it be autism," I prayed.

Kimmy finally walked at 25 months, but her feet were splayed and her gait was off-balance, a condition I later learned was ataxia. It was a morning in July when she was 2½ when Erin phoned me at my office with a diagnosis. I'll never forget the conversation.

"I've got some news about Kimmy, Mom, and I wanted to tell you right away."

"Oh, Lord." I sucked in my breath because her tone was telling.

"We saw a pediatric neurologist yesterday and he said he wasn't sure, but he'd lay odds she has Rett syndrome."

"What?"

"Rett syndrome. Like in 'Rhett Butler,' but without the 'h.'"

"What is it?"

"It's a neurological disorder. It's regressive, Mom."

With that word, the room went black and I struggled for breath, but it was like I'd been kicked in the stomach. I knew by then that with regressive mental disorders, the brain never recovers what's lost. Never. Not ever.

"It only happens to girls," Erin continued. "It starts around age 2 and they regress until they're 4 or 5, then they seem to stabilize. But by that time, they've lost so much. She'll never speak. And there are physical problems. A lot of girls lose the ability to walk. They all develop hand movements they can't control, like wringing..."

She went on and I heard, but my inner voice screamed, "My God, this is worse than autism. This is worse."

It was six months before Kim's diagnosis was conclusive and all of us who love her began to live with Rett syndrome. She grew physically, but she was able to do fewer things. At 2, she could stick plastic beads together. At 3, she could not. At 2, she could play chase around the dining room table. At 4, she could not. She couldn't even run. Not only that, she couldn't put together the mental synapses to play a game, not even patty-cake. The early days after her diagnosis were a time of grief and mourning. "We lost the child we thought we had," Erin said.

What has been triumphant, however, is the child who's emerged and the aura that surrounds her.

Kimberly Anne Dvorak is now 8 years old. Her condition is unchanged. She doesn't speak. She wears diapers. She can't grasp a pencil or a cup unassisted. Nevertheless, she is a reminder of just how precious life is and how profound the humanity is that resides within every person. I've never known a child easier to love than Kim. There is complete surrender on her part as there is complete dependency, and you learn that the surrender works both ways. The urge to give to this child is almost overwhelming and, as you try to teach her, it dawns that you are really teaching yourself.

Professionals think that Rett syndrome is a random genetic misfire. There are some 2,500 reported cases in the United States, but as it wasn't recognized by the American medical community until 1983, there may be 10,000 or more that are misdiagnosed or chronicled under "severe retardation of unknown origin." Women with Rett syndrome live a normal life span; however, as they get older, physical problems—including curvature of the spine, seizures, and the inability to swallow food—can threaten. A dominant characteristic is hand movement over which the girls have no control, such as wringing or washing. Kimmy claps her hands almost continuously. It's hard to know what's going on inside; however, it's clear that sensory information is scrambled. Only with intense effort, and only sometimes, can the girls pull themselves together to unjumble their input. It takes even greater effort to respond, communicating largely with their eyes.

We approach Kimmy with the understanding that there is a knowing person inside who just can't get out. The underlying philosophy is to reach for normalcy. We talk to her, include her, and expect things of her. Kim goes to school in a regular first-grade class in her neighborhood public school in Palo Alto. She attends in the company of a full-time aide, and lesson plans are adapted to her special needs.

Kimmy has likes and dislikes, hopes, dreams, and temper tantrums like any child. She loves Ben & Jerry's, Kraft dinners, and watermelon. She hopes when she comes to my house that I'll take her to the beach. She loves the ocean, has no fear of it, and laughs uproariously when the waves knock her over. She's addicted to *Sesame Street* and Disney movies and loves to listen to music—*Barney* songs, yes—but also show tunes where singers like Liza Minnelli belt one out.

I like to say out loud that Kimmy is developmentally disabled. I even use the words "mentally retarded." I want people to understand it's okay. It's normal. It's part of life. The first question often asked is, "Will she be in an institution some day?" thinking that will protect the rest of the family and will be best for the child. But the burden of these children doesn't chip away at love. While it's exhausting and can be overwhelming, it doesn't create the desire to shed the load. Rather, it stretches a person's own soul and enlarges the heart to accommodate. Erin and Rich would no sooner send Kimmy away from home than they would Peter, her precocious, fire-engine-toting little brother.

In the deep dark moments of the night, are there tears? And questions? Why me? Why her? Why us? There are no answers to those questions, and that line of thinking is a waste of time. As for tears, this is not a tragedy. In its own way, it is glorious.

I'm proud to be the grandmother of Kimberly Anne Dvorak as well as grandmother to her brother, Peter, and her cousins, Kevin and Casey.

But the one to whom I am grateful is Kimmy.

Edith

Joe Porias

Meredith Kaplan

*W*hat do you do with two wild-and-crazy kids who get engaged one month after they meet, and run off and get married just two weeks later? Well, if you're Meredith Kaplan, soon to walk down the aisle to marry the self-confessed love-of-her-life, Jesse Alexander, you listen to their marital advice. As it turns out, the "crazy kids" are Meredith's maternal grandparents, Edith and Joe Porias, who, despite their impetuous beginnings, have been happily married for 61 years!

Meredith, the lively, dark-eyed bride-to-be, regards her grandparents' matrimonial longevity as an enviable role model. "My own parents divorced when I was 2," she says, "so I grew up in a family of 'steps': stepfather, stepbrothers, stepmother. So there's a huge fear of...well...you know. Jesse and I recently got a dog, and we always say to each other, 'This is our family.' But sometimes, when Jesse's playing video games for two hours, I'll think, 'Oh, God, I can't take this!' Then I stop and look at all the other things about him and our relationship, and, of course, the good *totally* outweighs the bad. So, it's just reality, I guess. You have your own lives, then you come together in a marriage. Still, I have to admit, the longevity part is pretty scary."

In 1936, when Edith and Joe were married, there were many things to be scared of—the Depression and the insecurity of Joe beginning his medical practice, for starters—but staying together over the long haul wasn't a concern. "Back then, when you got married, you stayed married!" Edith says in the firm voice that often conceals her playful side. "Nowadays, *he'll* say something, and then *she'll* say something, and before you know it, that's the end of the relationship. We didn't do that. If we had anything to say, we said it, and got it over with before we went to bed!"

"For us, family was everything," adds Joe, who was an only child raised by a mother who'd been widowed when Joe was 9 months old. "Today, everybody's running around like flies all over the place. I read *People*, and this one's married three times, this one four times. What is this? Doesn't anyone stay married? It wasn't like that when we were young. You got married because you fell in love, and you stayed married through thick and thin."

And how did "love" enter Joe Porias' life? "I guess, in my mid-20s, there came a time when I thought it would be nice to be married. As it turns out, Edith's mother was a patient of mine, and I asked her how many children she had. 'Three,' she told me, 'two girls and a boy.' She said her youngest daughter was 19, and I suggested that she bring her around to the office next time she came for an appointment."

"My mother told me a fib to get me there," Edith remembers. "She said that she always felt sick after her therapy, and so she wanted me to go with her. I didn't want to go, because I had a date that night and a manicure appointment in the afternoon. But I was a good daughter, so I went."

"When I saw Edith walking with her mother toward the office," says Joe, "I thought she was very attractive, so I dashed off to change into my good clothes." After the appointment, the young doctor treated mother and daughter to a 35¢ ice cream soda.

"I was really annoyed," says Edith, "because I was going to miss my manicure. When we were leaving the ice cream parlor, my mother asked me what I thought about him, and I said, 'Don't ask me now, just get me home!' Who had a car in those days? We had to take two subways!"

By contrast, Jesse and Meredith met through a mutual friend, developed their own friendship, and went on to help each other through some serious romantic entanglements. "Jesse and I, at one point, had about four dates," Meredith recalls, "and took swing dance lessons together. But then he met a girl and fell madly in love with her and wound up proposing. He even asked me to go with him to an antique jeweler to help pick out the engagement ring! The fact that he was now officially involved with this other woman allowed me to let down a wall that I'd put up between us, as I had been thinking that he felt more for me than I did for him at the time. So, when he got engaged, I thought, 'This is great, now we can be terrific friends!' Which is exactly what we became, until he and his fiancée started having problems. Then, one day, their relationship ended, and the next day, we were together."

For Edith and Joe, getting to know each other really started once they were married. "We were total strangers, and, I often say, we were just lucky," says Joe, who gives a lot of credit to Edith, whom he describes pridefully as "a very good and enterprising wife."

She needed to be, as the Poriases subsisted on very little. "It was very difficult starting up a practice in New Jersey where no one knew me," Joe says. "I'd come home from the office, and, if it was a good day, I'd say to Edith, 'I had three patients today.'"

"Remember how much you'd give me to run the house?" Edith chuckles.

"I do," Joe replies, almost shyly. "One dollar a day."

"Thank God for Joe's uncle, the one who owned a delicatessen," Edith says. "Every week I'd make a shopping list and we'd go there to stock up. And no matter what, or how much, I bought, he always charged us the same—$10!"

So what about the 250-person formal wedding for which Meredith has spent months planning, and the first-class honeymoon afterwards to Bora Bora?

"Why not?" says Edith. "If that's what they want, and it will make them happy, they should have it!" That from a bride who looked radiant on her wedding day in a $35 rental gown, and who traveled with her new husband by bus to their one-week honeymoon at a rural farmhouse in New Jersey.

Years later, the Poriases traveled again, this time to follow their daughter, Meredith's mother, when she and her family moved to Canada. "We wanted to see the children growing up," says Joe, who nevertheless admits that it was difficult for him and Edith to leave their friends and lifestyle in Florida. "I tried to work in Vancouver, but I didn't really belong, and finally we moved to Seattle, where I felt comfortable practicing again." But when Meredith's family moved on to California, her doting grandparents followed once again.

If they hadn't, Meredith would lack the memories she now cherishes, such as the one about Grandpa's barter system. "Grandpa always wanted kisses, and if you asked him for anything, he'd say, 'That'll be 50 kisses!'"

And the influence of Edith, as the homemaker who could do anything, has perhaps led Meredith to wanting "a kind of Donna Reed lifestyle."

"I'm not a big career woman," she says. "I think my ambitions are more about having a nice home, learning how to cook well, getting the garden in shape. I think I'm an anomaly among my friends who are in the corporate world. But that's never been my place."

As evidence of her place—the devotion to home and family that she's inherited from her grandparents—Meredith is thrilled with her grandmother's engagement gift, a gold charm bracelet that reflects the milestones in Edith's life.

"I don't know why she wanted it," Edith says. "I told her, 'It's about my life, not yours. Why would it mean anything to you?'"

"Because it's all these things from your life, Grandma," Meredith answers. "When you were raising your kids, keeping your home. It's just beautiful, and I love it."

Jean Shrader

TJ Sharp

"*The farthest I'd ever traveled before were vacation trips to Mexico and Canada,*" says Denver, Colorado, grandmother Jean Shrader. "*But then, in 1994, there I was, sitting next to my 7-year-old grandson, TJ, on one jumbo jet after another, traveling more than 36 hours and 10,000 miles away to Vietnam!*"

Soft-voiced and thoughtful, Jean recalls the justifiable trepidation she had about the emotionally and physically arduous journey she had undertaken, and what it would reveal. "Not only didn't I know what to expect when we arrived there," she admits, "but I didn't know how I'd fit in, and what my place would be." As she customarily does in times of tribulation, Jean found solace in her rock-solid faith. A woman of deep religious conviction, whose conversation includes frequent references to God, prayer, and a divine plan, Jean does more, however, than just talk about her principles. She acts on them.

Her trip to Vietnam had its roots in events that had transpired almost two decades earlier. In 1975, Jean and her late husband, Frank, opened their home and hearts to three Vietnamese children who had been airlifted to the States following a wrenching separation from their family.

Months before, as the invading North Vietnamese neared their mountainous village, the children had fled with their father on his rickety motorbike to the main highway, where they were to wait for him to return with their mother and other siblings. As he reluctantly left his three children, their father admonished the oldest, a 10-year-old girl, Le Phit, "I will return! Whatever you do, stay together!"

Soon after he rode off, however, bombs began to fall and Phit realized it was move or die. Grabbing her siblings by the hand, she pulled them into the human caravan of villagers trekking south to Saigon. Constantly looking back, Phit yearned for a glimpse of her father, who had promised he would return to them.

In the war-ravaged capital, the children were placed in an orphanage where the youngest girl, 3-year-old Nga, fell critically ill. Now Phit was forced to make an excruciating choice: accompany Nga to America for medical treatment, or remain behind, hoping to be found by her father. Remembering her father's parting words, "stay together," the obedient child left with her siblings.

"At the time, we had three biological sons and two adopted daughters, one of Korean descent, the other of Vietnamese and African-American heritage," says Jean, describing her already full household. But, in a characteristic understatement, she adds, "All we had to do when we took in the children was put on an addition."

Some months later, when news arrived that the children's entire family had been killed in a bombing raid, the Shraders formally adopted the three children, Phit, Khoa, and Nga; changed their names to Heather, Jason, and Jenny, respectively; and proceeded to raise them like any other American kids.

In 1987, Heather was married to Denver native Tim Sharp and was the new mother of a son, TJ. Suddenly she was wracked with empathy for her birth mother, imagining how she'd suffered being separated from her three children. Heather's grief turned into an obsession that one or more of her Vietnamese family might still be alive. She decided she had to return to her homeland to discover the truth.

"We had always prayed for the safety of the Le family," Jean says. Yet, candidly, she confesses that her daughter's decision in 1990 to return to Vietnam to try to locate her relatives was extremely difficult to accept. "When an adopted child decides they want to find their birth parents, it's very emotional. There is a real grieving process. When we adopted the children, we weren't just baby-sitting them," Jean asserts. "They became our children."

After a fruitless first trip to Vietnam, Heather's hope diminished. But then she heard from an old family friend who promised to search for her family. One year later, word arrived that he had succeeded. Miraculously, the entire Le family was alive!

As soon as they could afford it, Heather and Tim, along with their third son, and Heather's brother, Jason, journeyed to Vietnam. Jean, who had recently been widowed, remained in Denver where she watched over Heather's two older boys. "Their grandfather and I had spent many hours with them," she says, "and built up a really strong, close relationship. The night before Frank suffered his fatal heart attack, TJ had been at home, crying, telling his parents that he wanted to spend the night with us. He did, and the next day, he was with me when Frank died."

Now, with TJ's parents halfway around the world, Jean prayed each morning for their safe return. "But then I had to get back to business and be a grandma," she says, "and make the boys their favorite breakfast, Swedish pancakes."

In 1994, a third trip to Vietnam was arranged, and now Jenny, the youngest of the three siblings, decided to go, too. "She had been so young when she left that she didn't remember her Vietnamese family," says Jean, "and felt unprepared for the earlier trips. But now she came to me and asked if I'd accompany her. I was honored, and told her, 'Of course I'll go.'" The "man of the family" on this trip was Jean's 7-year-old grandson, TJ, whose visit would fulfill Heather's earlier promise to her birth father that one day she would return with his oldest grandson.

After a day and a half of travel and several plane changes, Jean remembers arriving in Saigon (now Ho Chi Minh City) and being greeted by Heather and Jenny's brothers. "As I stared at the throng of people on the city's busy streets, I had to stop and ask God why he chose Frank and me to become parents to our three children. There had to be a reason," Jean says.

After two days of rest and sightseeing, Jean anxiously awaited their final destination, the Le family farm. "I just didn't know what I would find there," she says. Then later, after the tears and laughter of the reunion, and despite the expressions of gratitude from the Le family for Jean and Frank's love, care, and parenting, Jean remained disquieted. "Later that night, back in my hotel room in Nha Trang, I asked the Lord for his guidance," Jean recalls. "He answered my prayers, and thereafter I felt a great sense of peace."

Reflecting on the trip, and the courage and fortitude that it exacted from her, Jean says, "For TJ, I think it was just another adventure!" At home, Jean's favorite outings with her grandsons are much less challenging—trips to the mountains to visit relatives and afternoons at the Denver Children's Theater. But TJ's favorite pastime with his grandmother is even closer to home. "He loves to camp in my backyard and cook breakfast and dinner outdoors," Jean says. "Heather and her family gave me a tent for Christmas, and TJ figured out how I could put it to use!"

Indicative of her generous spirit, Jean didn't travel to Vietnam empty-handed. In Denver, she had assembled packets of hygiene products that she and TJ took to a local hospital, where TJ distributed the appreciated gifts to children suffering from burn injuries. "He is such a generous, sensitive boy," Jean says with pride. Clearly, he inherited by example, if not by genes, the attributes of giving, hospitality, open-heartedness, and caring that have made his American grandmother the special woman she is!

79

Saul Silverstein,

Michele Lee,

Ken Dusick

*D*ecades before receiving accolades for her role in the hit series *Knots Landing*, Michele Lee starred on a real-life cul-de-sac. This one, cherished more for its innocence than its intrigue, wasn't the creation of a producer or director, but rather the labor of love of Michele's visionary grandfather, Saul Silverstein.

"We all felt great on David Avenue," says Ken Dusick, Michele's brother/manager/best friend. His dark eyes, so much like those of his famous sister, sparkle when he recollects his family's early years. "We had very little money during most of that time, but I still felt we were the richest people in the world!"

"Oh, it was very classy!" Michele quips. "Kenny and I had to share a bedroom till we were almost teenagers!" In jeans and a T-shirt, curled up on the couch, her long legs tucked beneath her, the popular actress/singer's teenage days don't seem all that long ago.

"I finally did get my own room," Ken reminds her.

"Yeah, the *dining* room," Michele replies, breaking out into her contagious laugh, which soon starts Ken chuckling. Brother and sister banter a bit, in a way that only best friends can. Then Ken turns pensive.

"In one sense," he says, "David Avenue was a typical blue-collar neighborhood. But, in another, it was different from any place I've ever known."

This "different place" was the brainchild of their grandfather, "Papa," a transplanted New Yorker whose first order of business upon moving to California with his wife, Esther, was putting down $50 deposits on 20 houses on David Avenue, so that he could create a compound for the people he loved most.

"Listen to who lived on our street," Michele says, her hands delineating the imaginary block and houses that formed the neighborhood. "We lived here, Kenny, me, my mother, and father, Jack, who was a wonderful Hollywood makeup artist. My grandparents were two doors down and Papa's brother was between us. On the other side of our house were Papa's best friends from New York, my mother's sister lived across the street, and the rest of the neighbors were ex–New Yorkers."

"On July 4th, we'd have bonfires in the middle of the cul-de-sac," Ken says. "The street was a total anomaly. There were no light posts or fire hydrants, and it was never dedicated to the city. David Avenue was just a lost little haven."

"It was amazing growing up and knowing everybody there. Kenny, do you remember what we did if we were outside and we wanted a drink?" Michele asks.

"All we had to do was walk through any of the open front doors and get one," Ken says.

"Unless you went into Papa's house!" Michele reminds him.

"Oh, if you went into Papa's house for a drink, that was a whole different story. 'Grab a piece of fruit,'" says Ken in a lovingly funny imitation of his Papa's thick Polish accent. "'But, Grandpa, I don't want a piece of fruit.' 'Go on, have an apple.' So just to leave, you'd say, 'Okay, I'll have an apple,' and then he'd say, 'Here, have one, have two, have three.' You never left Papa's house with just one apple!"

Perhaps Saul Silverstein's indulgence of his grandchildren was a consequence of having forfeited his own childhood when he left his native Poland at the age of 14. Two years earlier, Saul

had joined a political activist group dedicated to overthrowing the czar. One night, after learning from a friend that all the group members were to be arrested the following day, he hastily scribbled a note to his parents and fled, leaving behind his younger siblings and everything he knew.

"He walked across Germany," Ken says admiringly, "and eventually made his way to England, where he became a clothing presser. He always said that he never got to see the sunlight, because he'd leave for work in a windowless factory at 5 A.M. and come back after it was dark."

"And he became a wrestler there, too," Michele says.

"He did? I never heard that, but I'd believe it," says Ken. "He was a really powerful man. Five-foot-five or five-six, and 210 pounds. Have you ever seen those Eastern European weight lifters in the Olympics? Well, that's what he was like. Solid!" Saul Silverstein lived to be 99, and, as Ken puts it, "sadly outlived all his children."

"Unhappily, we lost both our parents when we were in our 20s," Michele says, "and from then on, Papa was of paramount importance to us. Not that we wouldn't have been close to him, anyway. We would have, because that's the way we were brought up. But now he was our link to the past, and he became the center of our lives."

"He was a symbol of continuity for us," Ken says, "especially with our children."

Part of that continuity was learning more about Papa. Over countless breakfasts and lunches at his favorite deli or at his apartment, where he'd cook skinless chicken dinners in the microwave,

Saul recounted tales of his early life, often recorded on videotape for Michele's and Ken's sons and future grandchildren to watch someday.

"One of the most incredible stories about Papa was how he went back to Poland after having escaped to England seven years earlier," Ken says. "When he turned 21, he knew that if he didn't go back and enlist in the army, his family would be forced to pay a heavy fine. So, he went back, signed up, and spared his family the fine. Then he took the enlistment officer out to lunch, and while the guy was eating, Papa climbed out a window in the back of the restaurant and fled again. This time, he made his way to Antwerp and then on to America.

"So, he tells me one day over lunch, at a time when he's about 90 years old, that on the boat to America, he met this girl and fell madly in love with her. They get to New York, and he loses track of her, and it's driving him crazy because she's beautiful and he's mad about her. He puts ads in the Jewish newspaper to try and find her, but it doesn't work. Then years later, in Los Angeles, he's walking down the street, and he says, 'Guess who's coming towards me? The girl! But she was so old!' he tells me. 'I couldn't believe how old she was!' Can you imagine that? He's 90, and he's telling me how old *she* was!"

Deli lunches, holiday dinners, trips to doctors, and making sure that Papa had what he needed to keep up his independent lifestyle became part of the "parenting" that Michele and Ken, with help from their cousin Bernie, provided for Saul after their parents' deaths. "Our mother asked us before she died to take care of her father, and, of course, we did," says Michele.

Inevitably, there came a time when Michele and Ken began to worry about Papa's failing health. "I remember driving with him one day," Michele says, "probably home from a doctor's appointment, and I asked him straight out what he felt about death—not only to get his views, but selfishly for me, too, out of my own concerns about mortality. And he said he wasn't afraid of death. 'I know I'm going to die, and it doesn't bother me. I've lived all my life, I've done everything I wanted to do.' I think he had the perfect attitude, and it made me feel really good. You know, one way we learn about aging and accepting death is from caring for our parents, or in our case, for our grandparent. And I really got the sense from him that when you reach a certain stage of life, you accept what lies ahead. And that's always been very comforting to me."

Michele and Ken come together on the couch to look through Michele's wedding album, where Papa, wearing his usual hat, is prominently featured. "He didn't want me to marry Fred," Michele says. "He was sure he was too old for me, on account of his beard."

"And he didn't think I should marry Gina," Ken says, "because when she was 23, he thought she only looked 13!"

From the early sheltered days on David Avenue, Papa was always looking out for them, his adored grandchildren—the successful attorney, first in his family to finish college and graduate school, and his star granddaughter, whose *TV Guide* covers were proudly pointed out to everyone in the supermarket where he shopped. And then the time came when they looked out for him.

"We were his universe," Ken says simply.

"And he was our history," says Michele.

George Meyers

David Munk

heir relationship started out in textbook style: Grandfather nervously pacing up and down the waiting-room floor, in anticipation of the birth of his first grandchild. "What can I say?" asks George Meyers when questioned about his reaction to learning that his only child had given birth to a son. "Naturally, I was thrilled and happy."

But the 80-year-old lingerie salesman, whose contemporary style and spirit belie his age, is the first to acknowledge—to accept responsibility for—the strained way in which his familial relationships often progressed. "I was always so busy trying to be successful in business that I never was much of a parent to my daughter. I was never that close to her, even though at the time David was born I was living on the same block."

"That's not the way I remember it," says grandson David Munk, 32. The open, affable redhead brings a cup of coffee over to his grandfather and settles down on the opposite end of the couch, facing him. "I remember those years fondly, and think of you as being affectionate and attentive."

David's words aren't gratuitous. In the same painstaking way in which he created an exciting living space out of a dilapidated New York City factory loft, furnishing it with flea market finds, vintage photos, and nostalgic memorabilia, the talented record industry executive has labored to understand the uncommon dynamics between himself and his grandfather.

Meyers sips his coffee and shrugs—an honest man unwilling to take credit when he feels none is due. "I wasn't much of a parent," he reasserts, "maybe because I lost my own father when I was so young. I never had anyone to say to me, 'This is the way you do it.'"

As if growing up in the rough Brownsville section of Brooklyn wasn't difficult enough, young George Meyers had to survive the death of his father at age 7. "My family was so poor," he says haltingly, losing his composure in the telling, "that we had my father's funeral service in our living room. To this day, I can remember sitting outside on a bench, watching them carrying his casket down from our apartment."

"Mom says she thinks you never got over that," David says gently.

George nods, and wipes his eyes. "My daughter's a smart woman. A therapist. It's amazing how well she's turned out, because she didn't have it easy when she was growing up, either. My wife had a lot of emotional problems..."

"Nana *was* troubled," David says. "But I think the one place she succeeded in her life was in loving us."

"You're right," says George. "I know she loved you very much. But your mother was raised a lot of the time by her grandmother. Yet she was able to go on and have three boys, one after the other, and raise them by herself after her divorce. And you're all terrific kids!"

George also credits his daughter for allowing her sometimes-profligate father to come and live in her home when times were hard for him. "When my wife passed away, I got married again, but that didn't work out. Afterwards, I just threw myself into my business," explains George.

"In those years, subsequent to Nana's death, we saw more of you," says David. "I don't know if it was because you'd run out of money..."

"I started with no money, and I always worked with no money, and in the garment business you're struggling all the time."

"But there were periods when you had money," David says.

"And then I'd spend it," George replies.

"And then you'd get some more and spend it again," David says. "You were always in a period when you were either spending or struggling. I hope I'm better at saving money than you are!"

"Well, my philosophy is, 'You can always make some more,'" says George.

David laughs resignedly. "You lived your life pretty fast, Grandpa, which I can relate to. I don't want a slow life, either. I take chances professionally, which causes me great anxiety. But I'm an optimist. Are you?"

"I must be. I always thought I could make more money," George responds.

"Well, I remember when you didn't," says David, "when you came to live with us, sometime around 1976. I thought it was pretty cool then. I think that if someone called me up now and said they wanted to come live with me, I'd be horrified, but when I was young, it was a chance to have a father figure in the house again. My father was gone and we kind of liked having you around."

"I remember you coming to visit me, too, when I lived in Greenwich Village," says George.

"When you had some money," kids David. "I remember that. It was tremendously exciting. My first memories of New York City are because of you. Maybe that's why I feel so comfortable here. I'd come in on the bus from New Jersey and stay with you. We'd go walking through the Village, and I have memories of what it felt like, and what we did. We'd walk around, go into record stores..."

"Talking about record stores, I'll never forget what you did once. We had gone into a record store and you bought a record. We came out, walked a little bit, and then you found out that something was torn."

"The inner sleeve," recalls David.

"And you marched right back into the store, but they wouldn't give you back your money. So you started picketing outside!"

"I just wanted one without a bent sleeve," says David.

"They were going to call the police, but it didn't bother you one bit. You just kept walking up and down in front of the store!"

"Well, you always encouraged me to do what I thought was right. To take chances. You were never about playing it safe."

George nods. "If I wanted you to inherit one trait from me, it would be to do what you want to do, what you think is the right thing to do."

It may not be something that grandfather and grandson have ever articulated before, but each has acted on that shared belief, trusting that each would respect the other's choices. This belief was tested when, at a point during David's high school years, George learned that his grandson was gay.

"I'm trying to remember the exact circumstances of your finding out. Did I tell you?" David asks.

"Mother told me about it," says George. "Of course, before that I wondered. I'd ask her why you did things like go to ballet

school. Do you remember? I used to drive and pick you up there."

"You were always cool about it, Grandpa," says David. "You made a point of bringing it up after you found out. I think that's really exceptional, more so in a person from your generation than in someone of mine or Mom's. I look at you and see that you're not a judgmental person."

"I feel this way about it, David," says George. "I accept you for who you are. I look at your sensitivities, your warmth, your caring for other people, which you have much more than the average person, and I admire you. I respect you. The fact that you have different sexual preferences than I do doesn't enter my mind. I just don't care. All I know is, the first time I walked in here and looked around, I said 'Wow!' How did you have the confidence to know you could make such a fantastic home out of this place?"

"I think there's a genetic thread of arrogance that runs through the family. I've been taught to expect big things," David replies.

"Well, you won't ever give up! I know that," says George. "You're a part of me!"

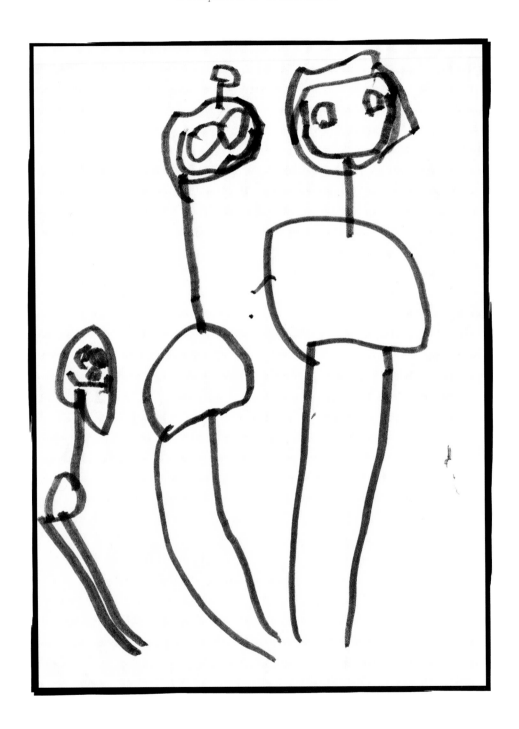

Anne P.

Grandsons

Two years after gaining foster custody of her two small grandsons, Anne P.'s adult son called her and said, "Mom, I'm picking up the boys tonight and having them sleep over. You need to go out and have a blast."

"I'm not a drinker," says Anne, whose lineage goes back to the earliest Mormons, "but I knew what he was saying. I was worn down and needed to get out and have some fun."

Anne made plans for the evening, but when the time came for her to leave, she couldn't. "All I wanted to do was cry," she said, "I missed them so much. It was one thing if I left them home with a baby-sitter, but quite another if they were not in the house." Indeed, Anne's two grandsons have very much come to belong in their grandmother's home, despite daunting adjustments and the challenges that still remain.

Taking over the care of her grandsons was not something that 44-year-old Anne ever imagined. Four years ago, she led a good life in San Jose, California. She had a job that paid well and close friends, and enjoyed teaching country-western dancing, selling Mary Kay Cosmetics, and especially living in her four-bedroom home complete with swimming pool. But Anne had also been touched by tragedy. She was twice-widowed, and currently estranged from her only daughter, whose boys she had not seen in over a year.

The oldest of those boys was the subject of a disturbing phone call Anne received one night from her son. "He told me that he'd just come back from a theme park where he'd run into my 5-year-old grandson, Teddy." [The boys' real names and their pictures are not used, and Anne's last name is omitted to protect their identities. "Josh" drew the accompanying picture of his grandmother, his brother, and himself.] "At first, Teddy didn't want to tell my son who he was with, but eventually he admitted he and his brother were living at the children's shelter, and they'd taken him to the park on a field trip.

"As soon as I got off the phone, I called the shelter. Since it was nighttime, there was no social worker to talk to. The man on the phone wasn't authorized to give out any information, but as I got more frantic, he tried to reassure me by saying, 'If they were here, they'd be doing just fine.' I finally reached the social worker in the morning and she told me that Teddy and Josh, the 1-year-old, were both there."

Anne hadn't seen her grandsons since her daughter cut off communication. "My daughter's life was in severe disarray, and I guess after giving her too many lectures she pulled away from me." When Teddy saw Anne at the shelter, he ran to her. "He jumped up on me and practically knocked me over! 'Grandma,' he cried, 'I knew you'd come!'"

Because the boys were now "in the system," only the court could decide their future. Anne promised Teddy that she'd see what she could do, and immediately hired an attorney to review the options.

One option was to place Josh with his father, who was not Teddy's father. When Josh's father failed to show up at a court date, Anne made a strong case for not awarding him custody in the future. She was so persuasive that the court-appointed children's attorney, the social service worker, and the deputy district attorney all agreed with her. "My lawyer took me aside and said, 'You don't need to pay me any more money. You can do this on your own!'"

Teddy's father was unknown, and now that she'd convinced the court about Josh's father, the question was open as to where the boys should go. "The social service worker asked me, 'How do *you* feel about taking them?' I hadn't considered it, but I said, 'I guess I could do it.'"

"Doing it" meant walking out of court with the boys, who had only the clothes on their backs. "On the way home, I stopped at the market for diapers. Then I thought, I don't have a crib! But it seemed a waste of money to get one when Josh was already a year old. So at home, I shoved the queen-sized bed in my guest room against the wall, and Josh slept on that side, and Teddy slept on the outside to protect him."

Anne scrambled to make the necessary arrangements—baby-sitters, school for Teddy, clothes and toys for the boys, much of which was donated by fellow workers after Anne's assistant put out an e-mail SOS.

What was the hardest thing about the first six months? "Lack of sleep," says Anne. "Josh has night terrors. It's not like nightmares where he can be comforted. With night terrors, he gets up screeching and then nothing will comfort him. My house was U-shaped, and I slept at one end and the boys at the other. I'd be sound asleep, hear Josh screaming, and I'd run down the hall, pick him up, and rock him all night. Sometimes, I'd sit on the floor and cry along with him. 'I can't do this,' I'd say. I never felt old until then."

Anne also discovered that many of her friends no longer felt they shared common interests. "People just dropped out of my life. I didn't like it, but I understood. I couldn't go out any longer; not only didn't I have the time, but I didn't have the money."

Eighteen months after gaining custody of the boys, Anne lost her job. About the same time, Teddy was having difficulty in school and started undergoing tests for dyslexia. When Anne called the school secretary to set up a test appointment, the woman looked over Teddy's papers and said to Anne, *"You're doing what I'm doing. If you're interested, there's a conference tomorrow on grandparents raising grandchildren."*

"Was I interested?" Anne says. "I couldn't wait! It was amazing to walk into this room with maybe 150 people there, all understanding what I was going through." After that, Anne joined a local support group, which helped her get through some of the most difficult moments with the boys—like talking about their mother.

"This year, we're writing a letter to the school to try and heighten the teachers' sensitivity to certain assignments. Like Teddy comes home at Christmas, or Valentine's or Mother's Day with presents for his mom. He asks, 'What should I do with this?' I decided to give him a box, and we keep all the presents in there. But that doesn't stop it from hurting."

Unable to find a suitable job in San Jose, Anne moved back to her old hometown and, for a while, moved herself and the two boys into her married son's small apartment. "There was my son, his wife and daughter, and the three of us—six people living in 700 square feet. It was very difficult. I tried desperately to find a support group, but the only one in the area had closed down years earlier. Just before Thanksgiving I made up my mind about what I had to do."

Anne contacted a local reporter and convinced her to write a column about Anne's situation, as well as on grandparents raising grandchildren in general. With a meeting place donated by Catholic Charities and a voice mail number to give out information, Anne waited anxiously for the first scheduled meeting—December 19, barely a week before Christmas.

"I had no idea if anyone would show up," Anne says. "It was during the worst rains we'd had in decades, not to mention all the things people have to do before the holidays. But that night 20 people showed up and they've continued to come ever since. Sometimes we have as many as 40, sometimes it's only three. But I'm really proud that we have five grand*fathers* as well as the grandmothers that come. One of the grandfathers is our treasurer; another is helping us attain nonprofit status."

And how are the boys doing? "It gets better all the time. At the beginning, when someone would think I was Teddy's mother, he'd grit his teeth and tell them, 'She's *not* my mother! She's my grandmother!' Now he corrects them, but without the anger. And Josh can go months at a time without a night terror, but then he'll have one, and we start over. One night I went in to check on him before I went to bed. He was sleeping so close to the edge that I moved him over, and inadvertently woke him up. I told him that I was concerned that he'd fall off. He just looked up at me and said, 'No, I won't. You're here.'"

Milledge Bryant,

Otis Bryant,

Brittney, Ashlee,

Derrick Bryant,

Elyse

Wesley

Bryant-Williams

When Otis Bryant was 8 years old, his grandfather, Milledge Bryant, gave him a tricycle for Christmas. "It was green and white," Otis recalls half a century later. "And I was able to keep it for a long time, maybe till I was 13, because I made sure I took real good care of it."

For Milledge, a 6-foot-tall, 200-pound farmer in Comer, Alabama, the gift was undoubtedly an extravagance meant to please his grandson, whom he called Sonny. "We all believed in Santa Claus back then," Otis recalls, "and for the longest time, that's who I thought brought me that tricycle. Then, of course, one day I realized it had to have come from my granddaddy."

In return, Otis loved to do things for, and with, his grandfather. "I remember sitting on the porch with him, being happy when he'd ask me to go and get him something. A glass of water, a towel, or the fly swatter. Many nights we'd sit out there, listening together to *The Grand Ole Opry* or *Amos 'n' Andy* on the radio. But it was a battery radio, and if the weather turned bad, we'd get so much static that you had to shut the radio off."

Today, Otis lives thousands of miles away from the corn, cotton, and peanut farm he shared with his grandfather. He and Oletha, his wife and childhood sweetheart, have a warm, inviting home in a well-tended Los Angeles neighborhood, where their five grandchildren, as well as the rest of the community's kids, come for help and advice, and sometimes a ride in Otis' two-door '67 Chevy.

On a spring day, before taking his two grandsons to one of their beloved Dodgers' games, Otis sits outside his home, flanked by his towering red and gold lilies, and enjoys the late afternoon sunshine. Surrounding him, as they often do, are his grandchildren, Elyse, 11, and Wesley, 6, who live next door with their mother, and Brittney, 15, Ashlee, 12, and Derrick, 8, who live with their parents only a few blocks away. Just as Otis shared his life with his granddaddy, these lively and bright children are now sharing theirs with him.

"We're over here a lot," says Elyse, beaming one of her ice-melting smiles. "Even if sometimes Grandma tells us we can't come and sleep over, we just ask Granddad, and he'll always say yes."

Otis can't deny it. "It's hard to say no to them, especially when they come at me with such charm. So most of the time, I'll just give in and say okay."

But that doesn't mean that Otis Bryant is a pushover. "We're trying very hard to work with the children," he says earnestly, never forgetting the first question Milledge Bryant always asked of him: "Have you been a good boy?"

And generally Otis was. "The only thing I can remember Granddaddy getting angry about was when I threw rocks," Otis says. "Then he'd threaten to whup me, but he never did. He was always patient, and I try to be the same with these kids."

Patient and present, as Otis finds time away from his jobs—house painting and driving for a film studio—to spend time with his grandchildren. "I can remember how exciting it was to go hunting with Granddaddy, and all the times he'd take me fishing. He'd bait my hook for me," Otis says, "even though every time he bent over, I could hear him groan. He was stiff and uncomfortable a lot from arthritis. I try to remember that, and move around a lot so that won't happen to me."

Little chance of that, as Otis works to keep up with his grand-

children's preferences and schedules. Although the girls are beginning to outgrow their passion for baseball and prefer shopping at the mall with Grandma, all the kids enjoy outings to the park and going to their favorite fast-food restaurants. Wesley likes helping his granddad paint houses, taking pride in the fact that when they painted his, "I only got paint on my shoes!" Derrick wants to be a DJ, and a ballplayer—so practicing pitching with his grandfather is routine. In addition, Otis and Oletha make it a point to attend each child's school activities.

But perhaps the best times are spent around their grandparents' home, where the children are kept in visual touch with their heritage through family photos prominently displayed on the fireplace mantel. Otis has also taken them back to Comer, Alabama, to see where he was raised.

"They were really poor!" Elyse says.

"And Granddad showed us the way he had to go to school," says Ashlee. "He had to walk, and it was so long!"

"It helped us learn the way things used to be," says Brittney. "We learned that we got it easy compared to how he had it. We've got it real easy!"

Otis acknowledges that his grandchildren live in a different world than he did, but he doesn't harbor any regrets about his own upbringing. "It isn't anything I feel bad about. Things went smooth for me. Whatever way it was, I learned to just go right with it. It wasn't bad, it wasn't bad at all."

But there were disappointments, like foregoing college

because of financial hardship. "Granddaddy wanted me to be a schoolteacher," says Otis. "When I was coming up, that was the best thing you could be." It's not by accident, then, that the Bryant grandchildren all are very serious about education and their futures. All express excitement and commitment about going on to college, for which Elyse—who, along with Brittney, plans to study law—has even begun to save. Distressed to learn that she'd have to pay for personal bills as well as tuition, she conceded, "It won't be so bad, if I just don't call my friends a lot."

To encourage their grandchildren's education, the Bryants have turned their back bedroom into a learning center. An IBM computer, programmed with reading and math games, sits next to a bookshelf filled with encyclopedias and Grandma's dictionary, which Elyse likes to read "just for fun."

It's getting closer to game time and the boys are antsy, afraid they'll miss the first pitch. Otis promises them they'll get there on time, taking a few last minutes for an admission.

"I didn't actually want to pattern myself after my granddaddy," he says, "because he was not an educated man. But, you know, the little education that he had, he used to his best, and I still loved him. He was a good person, and he always seemed to love his five kids and have a good relationship with them."

In a few weeks' time, Otis will return to Comer for a visit. Everyone there still calls him Sonny, just the way his granddaddy did. Maybe he will walk through the woods and remember the big man who wore suspenders and carried a walking cane that

came in handy to kill that occasional snake. Maybe he'll remember the gospel songs that Milledge whistled, and think of him when he takes the family seat at the Galilee Baptist Church.

But now it's time to leave for the game, and as his own grandchildren jockey around him and he laughs at their antics, he ponders what the single best thing about being a grandparent is. Before he can answer, Elyse beats him to the punch.

"Why, he's just happy that we were born!" she says confidently.

And looking at Otis' broad smile, you just know the girl is right!

American Memories:

May Lee Queen,

Carol Queen

Watt,

Donald Queen

To help provide jobs during the Great Depression, the government instituted the Federal Writers' Project, hiring approximately 6,500 indigent writers at a salary of $20 a week. Several of these writers, including Saul Bellow, Nelson Algren, Zora Neale Hurston, Ralph Ellison, John Cheever, and Richard Wright, went on to achieve international literary acclaim.

One of the assignments carried out by the project was the compiling of life histories of 10,000 Americans from various ethnic, religious, and occupational groups across the country. In reconstructing the stories from their notes and memory, the writers carefully reported the characteristic speech patterns and vernacular of their subjects, many of whom could remember back to the 19th century. Included in many of these stories were vivid recollections of grandparents whose lives helped form the fabric of our nation.

In 1938, in White Oaks, New Mexico, 56-year-old May Lee Queen told her life story to an interviewer from the Federal Writers' Project. Half a century later, May's Georgia-based granddaughter, Carol Queen Watt, discovered her grandmother's words in the Library of Congress' collection called *American Memories.*

"Reading my grandmother's story made me think about the tremendous changes that took place during her lifetime," says Carol, who is an avid compiler of her family's history. "As a 4-year-old girl, Grandmother traveled to New Mexico with her family in a caravan of covered wagons. Later, in 1914, she and my grandfather owned the first automobile in town. When I was a child, the first atomic bomb test took place not far from their home, in White Sands, New Mexico. From covered wagons to the atomic bomb, in one lifetime. That's a little 'future shock!'"

May Lee Queen's extraordinary life and lineage did, indeed, parallel milestones in American history, beginning with the arrival of her immigrant father, Captain John Lee. "He was born in Scotland," May began her reminiscences, "and came to America when he was 18 months old. At 14, he ran off to sea. He traded extensively in the South Seas, where he met and married my mother, the daughter of a missionary and granddaughter of Mataafa, the King of Samoa. My father sailed around the world three times and discovered a small island in the South Seas, which was named, in his honor, Lee's Island. When I was a schoolgirl here in White Oaks, I always felt very proud when we studied geography and our teacher, Miss Wharton, would show us the island on a map and tell the class that my father discovered it."

May, the next to last of Captain Lee's 11 children, was born in Virginia, but soon she and her family would join the great movement west. "When I was 4," she recalled, "we moved to Bracketsville, Texas, because my father always wanted to own a cattle ranch. There he met a man named McBee, who had a ranch at White Oaks, New Mexico. He told my father what great country it was, and so, in 1886, we headed there in five covered wagons. Father had about 200 head of cattle and 60 horses. I remember waking up one morning and hearing my mother crying. When I looked out of the wagon it seemed to me that all I could see were piles of dead stock all around us. It turns out the cattle and horses had died overnight from drinking the alkali water.

"We were a big family, and all the married ones settled around my father in the place that became known as Leesville. Father used to drive the stage to Socorro. I remember one time he didn't come home when the stage was due. My mother was very uneasy because the stage was often held up, and we were afraid that my father had been killed. He was a night and a day late, and just about the time my brothers and some neighbors got their horses saddled up to go out and look for him, we saw the stage coming over the hill into White Oaks.

"It turns out that they had run into a terrible snowstorm. My father and the passengers were almost frozen. He stopped the stage at our house and the passengers came in, got warmed up, and drank some coffee before Father took them into town. Father wore a beard, and I remember that it was all covered with ice and snow and you could only see his eyes."

On January 1, 1902, May Lee married a schoolmate, Edward Queen, and was living in White Oaks when New Mexico became a state in 1912. They had three children and two grandchildren, Carol and her cousin, Donald, who lives in New Mexico, not far from his grandparents' old home. Donald has heartening memories of both his grandparents and the life they led. "My grandfather was forced by necessity to become a man when he was only 12," he says. "He entered the mines, rose to the occasion, and was never bitter about his experience. He would later become a partner in a mining operation from which he would prosper. One of his two partners, Allen Lane, was the son of a Confederate supporter, while my grandfather's father had fought for the Union out of Ohio.

The third partner, David Jackson, was the son of former slaves. So it was an unusual, although successful, partnership!

"By the time I came along, the fiery nature of my grandfather's youth had evolved into the warm, steady glow of full manhood. He had a great love of nature, and I can remember wandering with him around the hills of White Oaks, and later San Diego, where my family all went to work in the factories during World War II. Children and animals would crowd around Ed Queen, as he was a kindly man. My grandmother, May, always seemed to have cookies, cake, or cinnamon rolls fresh out of the oven. Needless to say, they were excellent role models."

Carol, like her cousin, enjoys wonderful memories of her grandparents. "We all lived in San Diego during the war, Grandma and Grandpa across the street, and Donald and his parents around the corner. At Christmastime, Grandpa's old mining partner, Dave Jackson, would cut a tree and ship it off to me. I was probably the only child in California that had a personally cut tree from New Mexico!

"Although my grandparents lived in other places, they always returned to White Oaks—it was home. It was once the largest city

in New Mexico, but when I was a child only a few ranchers and miners lived there. Yet, when a dance was held in one of the old buildings, people from miles around would come. Everyone brought their whole family and blankets for the children, and all the ladies brought covered dishes. There were plenty of cowboys to play guitars and sing while people danced, visited, took care of the children, and ate.

"Grandma taught herself to play the piano and played in the Methodist church. I remember that she liked to play 'Zacatecas,' the Mexican anthem. She also sewed and crocheted, making a number of quilts, of which my mother still has one. She'd recite poems to me, one about 20 froggies that went to school down upon a rushy pool, that I wish I could find someday. She was a hugger. If I got away from her without all the breath being hugged out of me, I felt lucky."

When Carol was 11, May Lee Queen died at the home of her daughter in White Oaks. "I was there with the rest of the family," Carol recalls. "Grandpa had died a few months earlier of a heart attack during a family gathering. Grandma's last words were to him: 'Wait for me, Ed,' she said, 'I'm coming.'"

Grandma

&

Me

*P*laytime! A chance for 8-month-old friends to romp with their grandmas!

Harlene Sosin & Grandson Jordan Schore
"I think we share the same smile!"
"I want him to remember being happy with his grandma."

Pam Angel & Granddaughter Alexandra Angel
"Our baby pictures look just alike. Everybody thinks my picture is Alex in black and white."
"I want to do everything with her. I want to be her friend!"

Arlene Bromberg & Grandson Dylan Appleby
"I can't wait to travel with him."
"I want him to be a happy, helpful person."

Geraldine Kaufman & Grandson Sam Kaufman
"I think he looks like me!"
"I want him to have peace of mind, happiness, and be able to find a loved one. If he becomes president of the United States, that would be nice, too!"

E. O. Hoppé

&

Michael Hoppé

s Michael Hoppé leads the way into his marvelously eclectic home, he hastily explains that his immediate concern is finding owners for kittens he and his wife recently rescued from beneath their house. The handsome 51-year-old composer admits, in his native English accent, to having mixed feelings about parting with the feline orphans. "They're so cute now, but if we can't find homes for them, we'll wind up with a house full of cats!"

Such a playful menagerie would seem to fit right in with the charming decor—faded oriental rugs, overstuffed couches, bucolic watercolors, shelves overflowing with books and CDs, tabletops swimming with silver boxes and ivory carvings, and, of course, Hoppé's dark grand piano, which dominates the living room.

These Edwardian Era–like surroundings could easily have housed Michael's grandfather, the photographer E. O. Hoppé, who took the accompanying photo of Michael as a child. During the early part of the 20th century, the elder Hoppé was, in Michael's words, "the bees' knees." Cecil Beaton put it even more succinctly, calling Hoppé "The Master."

From 1908 until 1931, E. O. Hoppé photographed the most famous, accomplished, and aristocratic people of the period. The list of his sitters is awesome: King George VI of England, Pavlova, Clemenceau, H. G. Wells, Mussolini, T. S. Eliot, Sarah Bernhardt, Richard Strauss, Robert Frost, Mary Pickford, and Albert

Einstein, to name just a few. What distinguished many of his portraits is that at the time they were photographed, the subjects were on the cusp of fame. Such was the case with A. A. Milne, whose pipe-in-hand portrait was taken before his classic, *Winnie-the-Pooh*, was published. Hoppé's distinctive work always satisfied his belief that, "in true portraiture, no mere trappings can help in interpreting individuality. To confirm the spirit behind the eyes is the test."

With studios in New York, Berlin, and London operating simultaneously, Hoppé traveled extensively to keep up with the demand on his talent. "We didn't get to spend much time with Grandfather," Michael explains. "Even when he was at home, he was always disappearing into the darkroom." Their "quality time" was limited and mainly devoted to picture taking. "Grandfather would sometimes take me with him on country walks. He'd take his camera along, and I would carry a mirror, thinking I could capture the images with the glass in the same way he did with his camera."

E. O. Hoppé's dynamic and often difficult personality made it clear to his young grandson that their relationship would have to be on the older man's terms. "Grandfather had problems dealing with his family, as if his artistic temperament didn't allow him to have time for us. As for the role of children, it was definitely a case of 'being seen, but not heard.'"

Adults, like Michael's own father, Frank Hoppé, didn't fare much better with the self-absorbed artist. "I remember witnessing a very painful scene between my father and grandfather," says Michael. "My father was a senior executive with the Wrigley Chewing Gum Company. Once, after returning from a corporate meeting in Chicago, he came to visit Grandfather. It was a moment I'll never forget, as I watched my father, a demanding man himself, and physically larger than Grandfather, literally shrink in his father's presence. He stood before him, head bowed, hands clasped in front.

"'What is it that you do for a living?' Grandfather asked my father, in his German accent.

"'You know what I do, Papa. I work for the Wrigley Chewing Gum Company,' my father answered.

"'Chewing gum?' Grandfather spit out with disdain. 'You work for chewing gum? How can anyone do such a thing?'"

But as much as E. O. Hoppé disparaged the business world, Frank Hoppé revered it. When Michael's passion for music revealed itself, his father quickly saw to it that business, not art, would occupy his son's future. "My parents wouldn't hear of me being a musician," Michael says. "'Business, business, business' is what they instilled in me. At the age of 7, I was sent to boarding school, then on to Sandhurst, the British military academy, and then into the Army."

Eventually Michael established a stellar career with a major recording company—a clever way of combining his business acumen and his love for music. Fifteen gold and four platinum records later, the younger Hoppé had fulfilled his father's ambitions, and the time was right to confront his own.

"What happened next convinced me that there is no such thing as coincidence," Michael says. "Five years ago I got a phone call from a neighbor saying that he was looking through an art auction catalogue and came across a photograph of the famous dancer, Isadora Duncan. The credit for the photograph was given to one E. O. Hoppé, and my neighbor wanted to know if I was related.

"'Oh, yes,' I said casually. 'He was my grandfather.' Now, you have to understand that growing up, I did not appreciate my grandfather's work. I remember boxes and boxes of his photographs, with the edges all curled up, lying around the house. Maybe the way my father despised being forced to carry around Grandfather's equipment when he was younger, or because Grandfather could be so difficult, I never really gave his work the credit it obviously deserved."

Michael's neighbor gave him the name of the auction house and encouraged him to place a call to the curator. "When I told the curator who I was, he came right over."

There was an air of mystery about E. O. Hoppé, since few of his prints ever came on the market. "In 1947, Grandfather decided to give up portraiture and go into landscape photography," Michael explains. "I think he was tired of dealing with the idiosyncrasies of famous people. In any event, he sold most of his collection to a London-based agency. When I contacted them years later and tried to see the collection, the three partners refused to allow me in. I told the curator that he would meet with the same fate, and he did."

The curator persevered and, after the death of one of the partners, the surviving two decided to sell the agency, and the curator bought them out, brokering a deal in the process with Time-Life Books for more than 100,000 Hoppé prints.

When Michael Hoppé finally got to see all of his grandfather's work, he was simply overwhelmed. He was also inspired. Using his grandfather's portraits as motivation for his evocative music, Michael began recording his compositions in his living room, accompanied by either a cello, flute, or violin. Thus far, he has produced three stunning CDs, all paired with exquisite brochures featuring his grandfather's photographs. Ironically, back home in England, his father, Frank Hoppé, 85, now spends his time cataloguing his father's recently discovered portrait collection and perhaps coming to a better understanding of the man he never really knew.

"In a way," Michael says, "I feel that Grandfather is alive today. When I first sat down at the piano, and realized how his photographs could inspire my own art, I said out loud, 'Grandpa, we're on to something!' It's an amazing collaboration. Not only does his work motivate *me*, but I now have the chance to reintroduce his art to a whole new audience."

Michael puts on one of his CDs, aptly named *The Dreamer*, and contemplates the legacy left to him by past generations. "My father's insistence that I go into business helped me enormously. I wouldn't trade that experience for anything." As the haunting music fills the room, the playful kittens settle into a basket on the floor and fall asleep. "I could never deny my own art," Michael says, "just as my grandfather could never deny his. For him it was photography; for me it is music, and I shall do it for the rest of my life."

Grandma Moses,
Harry Moses,
Carl Moses,

Betty Moses
McCart

To the world, Anna Mary Robertson Moses is an icon—the quintessential depictor of rural Americana, who rose from obscurity to celebrity during the last decades of her long, productive life. But to her grandchildren, the primitive artist who created evocative masterpieces with five-and-dime-store paints and brushes is just Grandma—Grandma Moses, that is.

"I remember her redecorating a lot—painting rooms, wallpapering, things like that," says Moses' 80-year-old granddaughter, Betty Moses McCart. "I believe her first picture was painted with ordinary housepaint on a Masonite board. She wanted to make something to cover the opening in the fireplace." Now a widow, Betty still lives near the family homesite in Eagle Bridge, a village in upstate New York, within sight of the hills, bridges, creeks, and fields that dominated her grandmother's idyllic landscapes. Like her grandmother, Betty was a farmer's wife, and she, too, paints colorful, bucolic scenes of bygone days.

"People always think that the kind of life Grandma painted was picture-perfect, but it wasn't that way all the time," says Betty's brother, grandson Carl Moses, 78. Carl and his wife, Shirley, live and farm on the land where Grandma Moses spent the last part of her life, until her death in 1961 at the age of 101. The cheery pumpkins, plump tomatoes, and other produce they grow is sold at the Moses Farmstand, which is located just down the road from the one-story red brick house Carl built for his family. "I can remember when I was young," Carl says, "having to take a horse-drawn cultivator and work up and down the fields all day long. It was very hard work. I can tell you it turned me off of horses!"

But Grandma Moses (which *is* what her grandchildren called her so as to differentiate between their paternal and maternal grandmothers) did not portray the arduousness of farm life in her paintings. Instead, she conveyed its innocence—life the way she remembered it, or wished it to be. Amazingly, the diminutive woman in topknot bun, high-collared dress, and rimless spectacles, who once said, "I suppose I paint old things because I *am* old," did not begin her painting career in earnest until the age of 78.

"Before that, she was always doing needlepoint pictures and giving them away as gifts," says Betty and Carl's cousin, grandson Harry Moses, 60. A laconic bachelor who describes himself as "the last free spirit," Harry rubs his knuckles and says, "But then her arthritis got bad—I know for a fact that it runs in the family—and when she couldn't hold the needle anymore, she turned to painting." Enjoying his grandmother's dry wit, he remembers how she evaluated her choice of hobbies. "'I could have kept chickens,' she said, 'but I went to painting instead.'"

Grandma Moses was "discovered" by a New York art collector after she put several paintings up for sale in the drugstore window in neighboring Hoosick Falls. The small paintings were priced at $3, and the larger ones at $5. The savvy collector contacted her immediately and said he wanted to buy 20 paintings. "But Grandma didn't have 20," says Harry. "So she took the biggest ones down to the cellar and sawed them in half."

That was the kind of practical thinking Grandma Moses had learned and lived by from the time she was 12, when she was hired out as a farm girl. "She worked for a Dutch family who allowed her to go to school," says Carl. "They also told her that if she read the Bible from cover to cover, they'd give her a silver thimble. She never did go to church a great deal, but she knew her Bible and could recite passages from memory. And she kept that thimble until the day she died. It was a prized possession."

In 1887, Anna Mary Robertson married Thomas Salmon Moses, a farmer. On their wedding night they left for North Carolina, where the young bridegroom looked forward to escaping the harsh northern winters and buying a horse farm. "Because he was religious," Harry explains, "Grandpa wouldn't ride the train on Sunday. So they got off in Virginia, where he mentioned their plans to a man at their hotel. He told them that if they could wait one day, he'd take them out in a rig and show them some nearby horse farms. 'You don't have to go farther than Virginia,' he told them, and they never did." The newlyweds settled in the Shenandoah Valley and raised the five surviving children of the 10 born to them. Twenty years later, the Moses family moved back up north when Thomas grew homesick, and there they settled on land that remains in the family today.

"Grandma sold homemade butter and hand-sliced potato chips when they lived in Virginia," says Betty. "It was the first money that she ever made and she was always proud of it. I can remember eating big slices of her delicious bread, spread with her butter."

"She also made wonderful candy from grapefruit, orange, and lemon rinds, which she'd cook in sugar," recalls Harry.

"And she'd dry sweet corn and apples," Carl says. "In the winter she'd soak the apples and use them to make apple pies, which she served during the holidays."

"She made quite a lot at Christmas," Harry recalls, "when we'd all gather at her home." There were handmade gifts—mittens and a red-and-green wagon with black wheels that she painted for Carl. Betty recalls once getting a pretty stone from her grandmother on which she had painted the word "Moses." And a statue of a white horse that his grandmother gave him after he admired it remains in Harry's room at his brother's farm.

"She didn't have many pretty things when she was young," says Betty. "So everything attractive was important to her—a bright ribbon, or a pretty piece of paper." Even the most mundane items could find a way into this thrifty woman's artwork. One day, when a window frame fell off a passing caboose and onto his field, Thomas Moses picked it up and brought it home to his wife. "Mary'll paint on this," he accurately predicted.

Grandma Moses outlived her husband by 40 years. "I'm sure her painting helped keep her alive," says Carl. "Just like anyone else, if you haven't something to live for, you die."

"But she wasn't afraid of death," says Betty. "She told me once that when you die it's like the last moment before you fall off to sleep. You just don't remember it."

What Grandma Moses did remember were stories that she passed down to her grandchildren. "She said she loved to take off her shoes and run barefoot through the stream as a young girl," recalls Carl. "And she loved to do the things her brothers could do, like climbing trees."

And she also told them of historical happenings, like learning about President Lincoln's death. "My mother and I were traveling by horse and buggy from Cambridge to Eagle Bridge, and we noticed that everything was wrapped in black," she'd said. "Mother kept asking, 'What could this mean?' So, she went into a store and was told about the assassination. She came out and told me and we both felt so bad. But then Mother said, 'We can't help it,' and so we went on."

Many decades later, the famous artist who began as a country girl would sit with President Truman in the White House discussing farming, "just like he was one of my boys." She would paint over 1,500 paintings, be admired throughout the world, and correspond with President Eisenhower about his artwork. Yet she never forgot who she was or where she came from. "I look back on my life like a good day's work," she once remarked. "It was done and I feel satisfied with it. I was happy and contented. I knew nothing better and made the best out of what life offered. Life is what you make it, always has been and always will be."

"I don't think her success changed her all that much," her grandson Carl reflects. "But I think she sure did enjoy the attention!"

Diana An

Elizabeth An

iana An determined the fate and fortune of her family on the day that she decided to go on her first picnic.

"It was 1971," Elizabeth An, Diana's lovely, self-possessed, 31-year-old granddaughter explains, "and Grandmother was visiting San Francisco, the last stop on a two-month around-the-world tour." She glances at her grandmother, who sits beside her, regally dressed in a traditional mandarin-collared outfit of rich teal-blue silk. Her aristocratic bearing befits her royal Vietnamese lineage. She and her equally high-born husband have one son, Danny, Elizabeth's father, a former general in the South Vietnamese Army.

"In taking that trip, Grandmother was making a 'statement' to my grandfather," says Elizabeth. "He was an influential businessman and politician, with many women, as well as men, friends, dozens of whom he'd bring home unannounced to dinner at their French Colonial mansion. Grandmother had to 'give face' to Grandfather by presenting his guests with an elegant home and memorable meal. She worked hard at this job, spending seven days a week in the kitchen working with their three chefs—Chinese, Vietnamese, and French— creating new dishes so that no guest would ever experience the same menu twice. At least once a month, Grandfather would give a gala party for 100 to 300 people, which Grandmother would have to orchestrate. It was a continual job and very demanding work. Eventually, I think she felt taken for granted, and so one day, in 1971, she decided to 'make the statement' by leaving Saigon and traveling with her cousin to Europe, Africa, and America."

Diana An's "statement" unexpectedly led to the shattering of centuries of Vietnamese tradition, when she and her cousin chose to have one last American experience before returning home. They decided to go on a picnic. Stopping at a small San Francisco deli for sandwiches and drinks, they overheard the owner complaining about business to another customer. "He said he had invested $44,000 in the deli and wished he could now sell it," Elizabeth says. "Hearing him talk about selling suddenly gave Grandmother an idea. You have to remember, this was the early 1970s, when the Women's Liberation Movement was so prevalent. Grandmother turned to her cousin and said, 'How hard can it be to run this little place, when we serve 20 people without notice every night? Let's buy this restaurant, and let our husbands see what it's like when we don't come home.'

"Believing that a lady should not mistrust a gentleman, Grandmother told the owner she wanted to buy the deli, and agreed to pay the $44,000. But she only had $10,000 with her, which she would give him now, and pay the rest in installments. He quickly agreed to her terms. When she went back to the hotel and called Grandfather asking him to wire more money, he demanded, 'How much is this vacation costing, anyway?' When she told him what she had done, he immediately flew over to San Francisco to stop the deal, but it was too late. She had already signed the papers. Grandfather was furious, saying it was all the fault of the free thinking in America, of Christopher Columbus!"

Diana An looks down at her hands, clasped serenely in her lap. Although she has previously apologized for what she calls her poor English—which is, in fact, quite adequate—and although she says little, the small smile on her face reflects her understanding, and enjoyment, of her granddaughter's storytelling. Elizabeth takes a moment away from the story to editorialize. "I think you know now where all of the An women get our strength from!"

So how did a sheltered Vietnamese noblewoman manage to run a California deli? As Elizabeth asks that question of her grandmother, her tone is respectful and deferential. Diana's answer in Vietnamese amuses Elizabeth, who translates: "Grandmother says that she couldn't even imagine what a hot dog was when she began to run the restaurant! But very soon she learned how to cook American food, and little by little started to introduce Vietnamese cuisine, by placing a shrimp roll alongside a ham and cheese sandwich, for instance, to introduce the customer to the taste. People loved her cooking, and that's how the little deli she bought turned into the successful Vietnamese restaurant, Thanh Long."

Like everything else connected with their story, fate played an important part in naming the restaurant. Originally, Diana wished to call it Thang Long, which translates into "Ascending Dragon," the name given hundreds of years ago to the first capital city in Vietnam. However, when the menus were printed, an error was made, and the name came back as Thanh Long, which translates into "Green Prosperity Dragon." "Grandmother thought this was a sign from Buddha that we would be successful," Elizabeth says, "and so she insisted the name be kept."

But, in 1975, it hardly looked like the An family would ever prosper again. With her grandparents in San Francisco, and her father on a secret mission in Guam, young Elizabeth, her two sisters, and her mother, Helene, were imperiled as the Communists overran Saigon. "It was only the help of soldiers loyal to my father that saved us," Elizabeth says. "We were taken to an army base, then flown on a bomber to Guam, where we had an emotional reunion with my father." But, as the An family wealth was derived from landholdings, they had no assets to take with them when they escaped. Arriving virtually penniless in San Francisco, Elizabeth and her family joined her grandparents in their small two-bedroom apartment.

"It's hard to comprehend today the type of life we left in Saigon. It was very traditional French Colonial. A beautiful home lined with portraits of our ancestors, decorated with precious antiques and run with the help of many servants. As a child, I did not see that much of my mother or grandmother, which was the tradition then. Believe it or not, I had a little bell that I could ring, which would summon my nanny or my teenage companion, if I needed anything."

As traumatic as the move was on the An women, it was devastating for the men. "My father always believed the Allies would win the war and he, along with my grandfather, could never accept what happened. They suffered great depression and were unable to work for any length of time."

The fate of the An family now fell into the hands of the women. A path forged at a moment of whim by Diana An would be taken to limitless boundaries by her daughter-in-law and, ultimately, five granddaughters. "Mother joined Grandmother in the restaurant business, putting her brilliant culinary talents to work. I loved being able to spend time with them both, running into the kitchen and learning from them as I watched, and helped, them cook. Because I was always under her feet, Grandmother gave me the nickname 'Little Tail.'" Elizabeth went on to study fashion design, which she put to extraordinary use in designing the family's elegant seafood restaurants, Crustacean, in San Francisco and Beverly Hills.

Clearly, Elizabeth An, whose considerable entrepreneurial skills never subjugate her aristocratic heritage, is a product of two worlds. Rooted in America, she is nevertheless bound to Vietnamese traditions, and especially to Diana An, her Vietnamese grandmother, whom she credits with giving her the greatest legacies of all: her love of family, achievement, and personal independence.

Eulogy for

Yitzhak Rabin

By his granddaughter,

Noa Ben-Artzi

Delivered at the

assassinated prime minister's

funeral in Jerusalem,

November 6, 1995

On November 4, 1995, Noa Ben-Artzi went to hear her grandfather, Israeli Prime Minister Yitzhak Rabin, deliver the keynote address at a pro-peace rally in Tel Aviv. A former military hero, head of the leftist Labor Party, and serving his nation for the second time as prime minister, Rabin was now under bitter criticism from right-wing Israeli factions for recognizing the Palestinian Liberation Organization and establishing guidelines for eventual Palestinian self-rule.

"I didn't stay until the end," Rabin's granddaughter would later recall, "but returned home after Grandfather's speech. When I opened the front door, I was still so filled with joy and happiness from the rally, but then I saw my brother's face, and heard his words: '*Sabbah* ["grandfather" in Hebrew] has been shot.'" At the conclusion of the rally, as he was about to enter his car, Rabin had been mortally wounded by a Jewish extremist opposed to his settlement efforts with the Palestinians.

At Rabin's funeral, Noa delivered a heartfelt eulogy, providing a stunned world with a portrait of the hero as a grandfather, a man she adored and mourned, and to whom she paid eternal tribute with her unforgettable words.

You will forgive me, for I do not want to talk about peace. I want to talk about my grandfather. One always wakes up from a nightmare. But since yesterday, I have only awakened to a nightmare—the nightmare of life without you, and this I cannot bear. The television does not stop showing your picture, you are so alive and tangible that I can almost touch you, but it is only "almost" because already I cannot.

Grandfather, you were the pillar of fire before the camp, and now we are left as only the camp, alone, in the dark, and it is so cold and sad for us. I know we are talking in terms of a national tragedy, but how can you try to comfort an entire people or include it in your personal pain, when Grandmother does not stop crying, and we are mute, feeling the enormous void that is left only by your absence.

Few truly knew you. They can still talk a lot about you, but I feel that they know nothing about the depth of the pain, the disaster, and, yes, this holocaust, at least, for us, the family and the friends, who are left only as the camp, without you—our pillar of fire.

Grandfather, you were, and still are, our hero. I want you to know that in all I have ever done, I have always seen you before my eyes. Your esteem and love accompanied us in every step and on every path, and we lived in the light of your values. You never abandoned us, and now they have abandoned you—you, my eternal hero—cold and lonely, and I can do nothing to save you, you who are so wonderful.

People greater than I have already eulogized you, but none of them was fortunate like myself to feel the caress of your warm, soft hands and the warm embrace that was just for us, or your half-smiles, which will always say so much, the same smile that is no more, and froze with you. I have no feelings of revenge because my pain and loss are too big. The ground has slipped away from under our feet, and we are trying, somehow, to sit in this empty space that has been left behind, in the meantime, without any particular success. I am incapable of finishing, but it appears that a strange hand, a miserable person, has already finished for me. Having no choice, I part from you, a hero, and ask that you rest in peace, that you think about us and miss us, because we here—down below—love you so much. To the angels of heaven that are accompanying you now, I ask that they watch over you, that they guard you well, because you deserve such guard. We will love you, Grandfather, always.

Minnie Gonzales

Barbara, Pilar,

Gwyneth Thomas

When she was a teenager, Minnie Gonzales asked her father if she could go dancing. "No! You don't go and entertain everybody with your dancing," he told her, which was not an unexpected answer from a Latin father of the old school. The disappointed girl tried to reason with him. "I don't want to entertain *everybody*. I just want to entertain *myself*!" But Rosario Ayala had made up his mind. No daughter of his was going to go out and dance!

So Minnie made up her mind, too. She vowed that if she ever had daughters, she would allow them to dance as much as they wanted. That's a promise Minnie has kept not only with her daughters, but with her three granddaughters as well. They not only excel at jazz, but claim, over Minnie's denials, that they dance each night with their grandmother in the kitchen after washing the dinner dishes.

Just outside the kitchen, Minnie Gonzales sits in the quiet, sun-filled breakfast room of her daughter Alma's authentic Spanish-style home. As her fingers play with the colorful peasant embroidery on the tablecloth, Minnie apologizes for her memory.

"Lately, I forget a lot," she says, "so I don't know if I'm saying the truth or not. Things come and they go, and I wonder, is this a dream or is it real?" Something stirs under the chair beside her. Slowly, a furry gray cat pokes its head out, yawns and stretches, then retreats again into seclusion.

Minnie's frustration about her memory is contagious. One hates to think that this gentle, 83-year-old woman, whose lifetime has spanned such monumental changes, might not be able to remember and tell her opinion of them.

Minnie's life began in Mexico, but soon shifted to Riverside, California, where she moved with her family as a toddler. Her recollections of her native country are sketchy and embellished by what she saw later in the movies. "I remember a big church called the Virgin of the Rosario, because my father's name was Rosario, too. I also remember walking with my mother in a yard filled with melons." She pauses, removes her glasses, as if to readjust her vision, then replaces them, and sighs, "I think it was very pretty there, but I'm afraid that's all I know."

At that moment, Minnie's 16-year-old granddaughters burst into the room. Identical triplets, Barbara, Pilar, and Gwyneth are strong, graceful women; pretty brunettes with appealing smiles, chocolate-brown eyes, and a surplus of wholesome vitality. Their friendly voices sing out a chorus of "Hi, Grandma," as each runs for needed nourishment—fruit, Power Bars, and tall glasses of bottled water. Back from a two-hour jazz class, they are exhausted but exuberant.

"We're learning this great routine, Grandma," Barbara says. "We'll show it to you later."

"Good," Minnie answers, smiling, visibly perked up by the girls' appearance. As the triplets settle around her, each instinctively pats an arm or shoulder, or gives a peck on the cheek.

It's a challenge to tell the girls apart. When they were babies, each wore a different-colored pair of stud earrings, so that Alma and her now ex-husband, actor Richard Thomas, best known for his endearing role as John-Boy in *The Waltons*, could tell which baby was which.

In celebration of their heritage, each girl was given a Latin middle name, which Minnie offers to try to recite. "Let me see how good I can remember," she says, her eyes suddenly gleaming.

"Okay, Grandma!" the girls urge.

"Pilar *Alma*," she begins cautiously.

"Right, Grandma!"

"Barbara *Ayala*."

"You've got it. One more!"

"Gwyneth *Gonzales*!"

"Yea! Grandma! You got them all!"

Empowered, Minnie starts responding to questions that earlier eluded answers. Waxing nostalgic about her childhood in a camp for migrant fruit pickers, she especially remembers her school.

"It had a bell, and a teacher who I loved. I was learning English there, because we only spoke Spanish at home, and I remember this big Victrola, and the teacher playing a song I liked to sing, 'Beautiful Ohio.'"

Barbara: Grandma loves to sing.

Gwyneth: She used to sing in the church choir, and we'd go to hear her.

Barbara: And she was always singing at home, like if we'd say something, she'd say, 'That reminds me of a song,' and she'd start singing it for us.

Pilar: She still does that! When she watches TV, she'll sing along with the songs.

Besides a love for music, which the girls admittedly share

with their grandmother, were there any games Minnie remembers playing at school?

Gwyneth: Grandma, didn't you tell us you played baseball?

"I *did* like baseball," Minnie says. "And I remember there was a girl named Concha, who I used to admire so much. She was *such* a heavy hitter!" The triplets giggle at Minnie's description, causing Minnie to laugh at herself.

"What position did you play, Grandma?" Barbara asks.

"Catcher. I think I was a catcher," she says very seriously.

"Good for you, Grandma," says Barbara. "You are so cool!" Her sisters agree. Triple A approval.

And what did Minnie think when she found out that Alma had given birth to triplets? As Minnie begins to answer, a Great Dane puppy enters the room, with Alma close on its wayward heels.

"Well, my mother had twins," Minnie recalls, "so I thought it runs in the family."

"Do you want to know what you *really* said when I told you there were three?" Alma asks, cornering the Shetland pony–sized dog.

"What did I say?" asks Minnie.

"You said, 'I never *heard* of such a thing!'"

Minnie bursts out laughing. "Oh, but I was so happy! Imagine, having *three* girls!"

Three girls to love, and three girls to love her.

"I think we all share Grandma," Gwyneth says. "We've never felt like we had to compete for her love or attention, because she's always handed it out equally."

"Which is a cool thing when you're a triplet!" adds Pilar.

Minnie has always offered help with the girls whenever it has been needed. "Grandma's always tried to protect us," Gwyneth says. "She tells us when we go out, 'Be careful. If someone offers you a drink, they might put something in there, and you will not be able to take care of yourself.'"

Minnie adds, "Things are so different now than when I grew up. Instead of going to school at their age, I had to pack oranges to make money. Today is very different. I cannot say it's not good. It's just different. But I *do* say, 'Be careful.'"

In her protective way, Minnie now acts like her own well-intentioned father who forbade her from dancing so long ago.

As Barbara puts on a '40s Big Band CD, Gwyneth and Pilar urge Minnie to come and dance with them.

"Okay, okay," Minnie says, eager but not about to be rushed. "Give me a minute," she says, smoothing the front of her blouse. "I'm waiting for the beat."

Dorothy Bundy

Cheney

Andrew Cheney

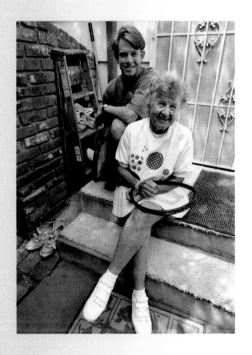

heir blue eyes are the color of the sparkling Pacific Ocean, which shines through the pines and palms surrounding Dorothy ("Dodo") Cheney's La Jolla home. As the vivacious grandmother and her 21-year-old grandson, Andrew, sit in Dodo's cozy living room talking about the town, their family, outdoor life, and each other, the happy pair reminisce and laugh. They have good reason to do a lot of both.

Dodo Bundy Cheney is, in Andrew's apt words, "unique." Born in 1916 to an affluent Los Angeles real estate developer and his tennis champion wife, Dodo (nicknamed by her younger brother who couldn't pronounce Dorothy) radiates vitality and vigor. The silver trays, bowls, trophy cups, and plaques throughout her inviting home are a testament to her championship spirit and philosophy.

"I believe you should have lots of interests. Always be doing something, whatever it is that appeals to you. As you get older it's especially important to keep your mind and body going," Dodo says. And "go" she does. Her days are gloriously filled with gardening, surf fishing, golf, sewing, croquet, travel, jigsaw puzzles, acrostics, friends, family, and, of course, her beloved tennis.

Dodo Cheney is a tennis phenomenon, having won more tennis championships than any other player in U.S. history. The United States Tennis Association has awarded her an unprecedented 269 gold-plated miniature tennis balls for her national title wins in a gamut of tournaments ranging from amateur to professional, junior to senior. Including her major win in the 1938 Australian Open, Dodo has won 20, maybe 30, Grand Slams. "I'll have to count one day to make sure," she says unassumingly.

"That's just like Dodo," says Andrew, who knows that for his grandmother, winning always comes second to good sportsmanship.

"They're the things I'm most proud of," she says, speaking of her sportsmanship awards. "I know Brian [Dodo's son, and Andrew's father, a teaching pro in Phoenix] has won several of them, too."

"I won two last year, Dodo," Andrew adds with quiet modesty. Andrew, a student at UC Irvine on a tennis scholarship, is the fourth generation of tennis champions in his outstanding family. His great-grandmother, May Sutton Bundy, was America's youngest tennis champion. She and her husband, Thomas, also a champion, founded the prestigious Los Angeles Tennis Club. Andrew believes that "sportsmanship genes" were passed on from Dodo to his father, and then down on to him. "It's expected in our family," he says.

"Now, that's more important for me than winning!" says Dodo. "Being a good sport! If you're a good sport in athletics, then you're inclined to be a good sport in life. A good mother, a good father, a good husband, a good wife." Her eyes take on a mischievous twinkle, as she adds, "But did I tell you, Andrew, that I played in a tournament last week at the club and we won!"

"That's great, Dodo," Andrew responds, his handsome, tanned face breaking into a broad smile.

"And," Dodo says, her blond curls bouncing as she chuckles, "I developed a new name for my drop shot. The 'stinky dink!'" Grandmother and grandson laugh together, as they've done for as long as Andrew can remember.

Dodo and her late husband, Arthur, a pilot for Western Airlines, raised two boys and a girl who produced eight grandchildren. "One of my first memories of Dodo is being at her log cabin in Rustic Canyon in Santa Monica," Andrew recalls. "It was a kid's paradise. There were so many of us running around that she had to put two big chairs together to make a bed for me. And all the babies used to get washed in the kitchen sink. But the best part of it was the way the house smelled. It was just a Dodo smell—she still has it when you get close to her. I don't know if she got the smell from the cabin or the cabin got it from her, but it makes me think of being in the kitchen with her, having her make me the world's best poached eggs!"

And then, of course, there were the inevitable outdoor activities. "Remember, Dodo, how you taught me to surf fish?" Andrews asks.

"Oh, yes, but it was trouble teaching you to cast. If you didn't get everything just right with those old-time reels, it could be such a mess. And you insisted on casting for yourself; you didn't want me to do it for you. So you wound up spending a lot of time untangling your line, as I remember!"

Fishing is just one of the passions that grandmother and grandson share. To keep up with her grandson, Dodo has even tried her hand at tackle football. As long as the activity is fun and competitive, she's willing to give it a go.

"A couple of years ago, we teamed up and really became

tough to beat in croquet," Andrew says. Beach croquet is one of the hotly contested events at the annual July reunion of Cheney cousins at the La Jolla Beach and Tennis Club.

"Tell about the obstacles, Andrew," Dodo urges, her eyes bright with amusement.

"Oh, Dodo and I make it tough for the others," he says. "We put seaweed around the hoops and dig little holes in the sand."

"We have so much fun, don't we, Andrew?"

Fun is essential to Dodo Cheney. "I do believe that laughter is the best medicine," she says. "When you get older, you inevitably lose your mobility, your speed, your eyesight, but you can still get out there and have fun, and even win, using control and tactics." Some of her tactics include finding ways of remaining competitive with Andrew as his tennis game grew to surpass hers.

"Dodo used to beat me all the time when I was little," he says. "But then, as I got older, the court seemed to get bigger for her and smaller for me."

"I used to make up all sorts of rules so I could still win," Dodo laughs. "Like letting me hit on the second bounce, or making him serve underhanded, or letting me play the alleys. But now I just love watching him play. My mother used to get so nervous when I would play that she couldn't watch."

A wonderful portrait of the lovely May Sutton Bundy hangs above the fireplace. The resemblance between mother and daughter is uncanny. "Sometimes Mother would have to hide behind a tree so she wouldn't see me," Dodo says. "But I just love

to watch the game. If Andrew wins, fine, and if not, not."

Andrew devotes a lot of time, however, to making sure that he remains on the winning side. In addition to a part-time job, friends, and a full load of civil engineering courses, he is on the court practicing his tennis five hours a day. After graduation, he hopes to make the pro tour. After that, an MBA. Clearly, he's infused with the Cheney philosophy of activity and accomplishment. For these attributes, he credits not only his devoted parents, but also Dodo. "From her I learned to have a zest for life, to work hard, to do a lot, to be respectful, and be a good sport. She's been through a lot, growing up in a wealthy family, then being hit, like everyone else, during the Depression. She knows how to be frugal but always generous. She drives a Lexus sports coupe to her tournaments, but everywhere else she runs around in her 20-year-old beat-up El Camino!"

Dodo politely interrupts. She's running late. Friends are waiting. She checks to make sure she's wearing her signature pearl choker, earrings, and triple-strand bracelet. Does she have her large sunglasses and headband tucked in her gold lamé tote bag? Later in the day, she'll return home to tend to her squash, figs, flowers, and lemons; work on the thousand-piece jigsaw puzzle awaiting completion on the dining room table; bake one of her famous rum cakes; and finally finish that pleated tennis skirt she'll wear in an upcoming tournament.

Andrew appears undaunted by his grandmother's astounding energy. But then again, you have to remember, he's a Cheney. And for them, it comes naturally.

Suzanne

Lafond

Mary, Morgan,

Sara Stengel

On May 1, 1997, Suzanne Lafond was in Wenatchee, Washington, far from her Nashville, Tennessee, home, doing something she'd never done before: riding in a parade. Perched on the seat back of an antique Ford convertible, Lafond and two other women seated behind her in the rumbleseat were among 20 finalists in the Washington State Apple Commission search to find "the world's greatest granny." The winner, Granny Smith 1997, would travel throughout the country on behalf of Washington apple growers, promoting good nutrition and an active lifestyle for seniors.

"I was amazed at the turnout," Suzanne says with an engaging southern lilt. "Over 60,000 people came for the Apple Festival, a hugely popular event in the Northwest." Chuckling, she adds, "At one point, we rode past three young men who yelled out, 'Hey, that car's older than you are!' 'No, it's not,' I yelled back. 'We're twins. It's a 1931!'"

Throughout the day, Suzanne enjoyed the crowd's enthusiasm, the judges' interviews, her accomplished fellow contestants, and the support of her childhood friend, Marlene Pinck, who'd flown in from their hometown of Montreal, Canada. But later, when Suzanne was picked as one of the 10 semifinalists, anxiety and doubt set in. "It dawned on me that I *really* wanted to be chosen," she says. "I wound up saying to myself, 'Suzanne, just *who* do you think you are? You don't have a chance!'"

That opinion was definitely not one shared by her two oldest granddaughters, Morgan and Mary Stengel. Months earlier, while food shopping in a Nashville market, the sisters, aged 10 and 12 respectively, had seen a display for the contest and decided to enter Suzanne, whom they call *Mamie*. A French term of endearment, Mamie is a contraction of *bon amie*, or dear friend. "It's what my three sons called my mother," Suzanne explains, "and I wanted my four granddaughters to call me that, as well."

Following the contest instructions, the girls wrote letters outlining why they felt their grandmother was "the world's best." As well as describing her as "sweet," "loving," and "generous," Morgan mentioned that Suzanne is "very modern"—a match with the Apple Commission's mandate to find "a granny-on-the-go." Closely involved with family and friends, busy with her multiple careers and avocations, it would be difficult to find someone more active than Suzanne Lafond.

"When I turned 60, I realized that I needed to find a way to look after myself and never be a burden to my sons," Suzanne, a divorcée, says. "If you had told me 10 years ago that I'd be selling long-term health insurance, I would have laughed. But here I am doing just that, and I really feel that I'm doing something helpful, especially for widows who have never worked and really don't know what to do when they're suddenly left on their own."

Suzanne's attractiveness and grace make her a natural for modeling in commercials and print work and acting in training films and voice-overs. "I really enjoy that work," she admits, "but it's not a career that you can rely on."

As if two demanding occupations aren't enough, she is also a fitness buff. An aerobics "pioneer," she's faithfully exercised three times a week for the last 18 years. More recently, she's taken up power yoga, step classes, and jogging. This past year, she and her granddaughter Mary ("christened Mary Elizabeth," Suzanne says, "but in first grade with her big handwriting, 'Mary' was all she could fit on her library card!") both took first place in their age divisions in a 5K race.

"Mary, Morgan, and their 6-year-old sister, Sara, are all athletically, academically, and artistically gifted," Suzanne says proudly. "I love having them over to my house on Saturdays. Whether we're just playing board games at home, or on a bleak winter afternoon going to the science museum and learning something new, it's always fun to be with them. I also enjoy shopping with the girls, and I'm especially delighted that Mary, who's almost a teenager, likes to go clothes shopping with me. I think my modeling work helps to give me a sense of what the younger generation is wearing, and maybe even be more accepting about it than her parents are. Not that I'd want to see her with a bare midriff, mind you, but when you're a teenager you certainly don't want to look like a dork!"

Suzanne also adores the girls' new baby girl cousin, August Stengel, for whom she helps to provide daycare. "I just think that babyhood is so wonderful," she says, "and I'm delighted to help out so that my daughter-in-law can return to work."

Suzanne lauds her sons and daughters-in-law. "The girls are all very lucky. They have wonderful parents from whom they get tremendous support. But I can provide support, too, and also somewhat of a different perspective. As a grandparent, I find I'm not so overwrought about everything. Plus, I've had 20 to 30 years of life experience that I didn't have when I was a parent, and a lot more patience!"

But at the Granny Smith competition patience was in short supply as Suzanne waited to hear the judges' decision. Then the celebrity host, Shirley Jones, made the grand announcement. Out of 8,000 entrants from the United States and Canada, Suzanne Lafond was chosen as Granny Smith 1997! "I don't like to think of it as winning," Suzanne says, "because that makes it seem as if the others lost, and they were such outstanding women."

Suzanne isn't sure what gave her the edge, but she recalls a moment in the video she submitted that seemed to engage the audience. "The three older girls were all in the video," Suzanne says, "and at one point, Sara became moody, and I instinctively began to sing her a little French lullaby. I don't know why. I guess I just thought it would be soothing. So when my name was announced and I went up to accept the award from Shirley Jones, she said to me, 'I wish I could speak French.' And I said to her, 'I wish I could sing!'"

By the time Suzanne called home with the news, a local TV station was already on its way to her oldest son's home to interview the family and get their reaction. Suzanne's second phone call was to her brother, Pierre, a gourmet food and wine retailer in Santa Barbara, California. "I thought he might razz me,"

Suzanne says, "but he was thrilled. His first question was, 'Do they know how much we love apples?' I told him that I hadn't said anything about that, thinking it might seem insincere. But you know, we really *do* love apples. We always have!"

What else would you expect from Granny Smith?

Maggie Schneidewind

&

Benjamin Salisbury

"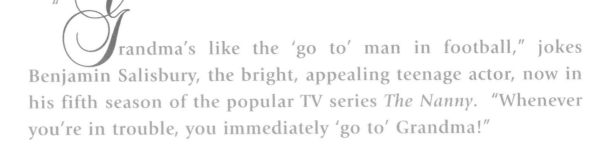randma's like the 'go to' man in football," jokes Benjamin Salisbury, the bright, appealing teenage actor, now in his fifth season of the popular TV series *The Nanny*. "Whenever you're in trouble, you immediately 'go to' Grandma!"

Benjamin's safeguard, his maternal grandmother, Maggie Schneidewind, is a buoyant red-head who adores being "Nana," a role she coveted ever since she was a small girl. In the Marina del Rey apartment that Benjamin, his mother, and younger brother, Jacob, use as a home base while *The Nanny* is in production, Maggie explains her devotion to grandparenthood.

"My parents got married when they were young, too young," she says, "and although they were deeply in love, their marriage just didn't work out. So my mother—who was more like a big sister to me—and I went to live with my maternal grandparents. They raised me and gave me such a loving, great childhood that I vowed if I ever had grandchildren of my own, I would give them the same kind of love and care that I had received from them."

Like her grandson, Maggie is a native of Minneapolis. In the early 1960s, she and her late husband, Merle, sold their family home and moved to San Diego. "My children were so upset with me for selling the house," she says, "but my grandchildren have a different attitude. They always say to me, 'Grandma, wherever you are, that's home!'" Today, Maggie's nine grandchildren (Benjamin is the seventh, and was the first grandson) are scattered around the country, a costly arrangement since Grandma supports carte-blanche communication.

"Benjamin's mom was a single parent of four for most of the time, and so we were very involved," says Maggie. "We wanted to put some stability in the children's lives, and so we told them they could call us whenever they wanted—collect."

"So we did, whenever we had a fight," laughs Benjamin.

"Or wanted me to intercede with your mom!" laughs Maggie, who characterizes herself as "a buffer" in disagreements between her children and grandchildren. "I don't see it as interfering, not the way it would be if I were trying to settle a dispute between a husband and wife," she says. "If I agree with the kids, I'll call up my son or daughter and tell them what I think—although I'm not sure if it helps to change anything."

"Oh, it does, Grandma," Benjamin assures her. "Ninety-eight percent of the time, Mom changes her mind."

With that average, it's not surprising that Benjamin calls his grandmother practically every day. "She's taking care of Sassy, one of our cats, so we need to call her and check up on him."

Pictures of Sassy, as well as other family pets living back home with Benjamin's stepfather; a photo taken by Benjamin of his mother's beloved Minneapolis rose garden; a mountain of stuffed animals in Jacob's bedroom; and Benjamin's favorite pastimes—chess, Scrabble, and shelves of books—add personal touches to the otherwise generic apartment, the kind of temporary living arrangement that's part of a working actor's life.

"We're going to Grandma's for Thanksgiving," Benjamin says enthusiastically. "Now that's home!"

Benjamin first visited his grandparents in San Diego when he was only 2 months old. "I worked for the county in public relations for 23 years, and each year I would take my vacation time at home with the family," says Maggie. "Since everyone's schedule was different and we couldn't get together on Christmas, I'd fly everyone out during the summer, and we'd celebrate the holiday then, all of us together with more presents than you can believe!"

Benjamin vividly remembers his first solo trip to San Diego when he was 9. "I felt very independent, going so far. I stayed for two weeks, but it seemed like forever. It was the greatest time.

"While I was there, the Padres had a nine-game home stand, and every day Grandpa took me to the game and we sat behind home plate. He'd give me a $20 bill and say, 'Go get two of something.' I remember asking him, 'Can I get two beers, Grandpa?' 'NO!' he said. So, I came back with two hot dogs and two sodas, and then I wanted something else, and it was another 20 bucks. At the last game he said, 'I'm NEVER going to another baseball game again!'"

"Merle loved sports," recalls Maggie, "but after Benjamin left, he asked me, 'When's he coming back again? I've got to rest up!'"

Another of Benjamin's favorite memories is the trip he took with Maggie to Washington, D.C. "When we graduate from elementary school, Grandma takes us on a trip of our choice..." begins Benjamin.

"Anywhere in the continental United States," adds Maggie. "I've been to Disney World twice, Six Flags, Universal Studios, and the Mall of America! Benjamin and his sister both decided they wanted to go to Washington, D.C."

"It was so much fun," remembers Benjamin. "We had lunch in the Senate dining room, met Senator Kennedy..."

"And your own senator from Minnesota," reminds Maggie.

"I was really into the political scene then," says Benjamin. "President Bush had recently come to Minneapolis and visited my school, which was the first to utilize the Internet. For some reason, that got me interested in politics."

"Benjamin is very smart," his proud grandmother says. "He just loves reading. When he was 6, and Jacob had just been born—I think he was only about 4 days old—I called to see how everyone was doing. Benjamin answered and said he was reading to Jacob from *Reader's Digest*!"

"I remember I loved the military jokes," Benjamin laughs. "I thought they were so funny."

"So I asked him when he might start reading Jacob nursery rhymes, and Benjamin thought for a minute then said, 'Maybe when he's about 6 months old.'"

Maggie also shares a close rapport with Jacob, after coming to the rescue when Benjamin was given a last-minute opportunity to act in a feature film.

"We were in Minneapolis, and got a call around midnight offering me the role in *Captain Ron*," says Benjamin. "My step-father works seven days a week, so he couldn't be home with Jacob, and my mom had to accompany me to Puerto Rico for the shoot. So we called Grandma, and, of course, she said, 'Send Jacob to me!' So six o'clock the next morning, my mom and I put Jacob on a plane to San Diego, and we flew to Puerto Rico.

"I was really lonely for Jacob," says Benjamin, "especially when it was his birthday. Mom and I called, sure that he was miserable being without us, and I said, 'Hi, Jacob, it's Benjamin!' and he said, 'Oh, I remember you!' He broke my heart! Then he said, 'I'm hanging out with Grandma and Grandpa, and we're ready to cut my cake. So I've gotta run. If you're going to sing "Happy Birthday," sing fast!' He just cracked me up!"

"My grandchildren have always been surrounded by their grandparents," Maggie says. "I think that grandparents are the ones who can teach their grandchildren to be kind and respectful of elders. All my grandchildren have gone into nursing homes and chatted with the folks, putting a little bit of happiness into someone's life who doesn't have any family. I just want my grandchildren to be good human beings."

On that score, it's clear that Benjamin's success hasn't spoiled him. He is gentlemanly and amiable and unspoiled by success. He loves doing the series, which has become a family affair, with his late grandfather doing a voice-over in one episode and his brother playing Benjamin as a young boy in a flashback. While he hopes the show is renewed, he admits, "It's not my whole life." Benjamin looks forward to college, maybe even law school. His grandmother listens to his plans and nods, a staunch supporter always in his corner.

"I don't worry about the business, about getting jobs and being rejected," Benjamin says. "Grandma's given me some good advice: Don't burn your bridges, be honest with yourself, and do the best you can. I think I'll just listen to her."

Ann Lipsman

Natalie Schachner

nn Lipsman sits at one end of her sofa recounting her four years in Nazi concentration camps. At the other end is her pretty granddaughter, 16-year-old Natalie Schachner. As Ann tells of her devastating experiences, Natalie instinctively edges closer.

In front of them, on a coffee table, is a composition Natalie wrote for a school project.

I always look forward to weekends when I sleep at Grandma's. I walk into her warm apartment where the door is open wide because she knows I am coming, and run into her big arms and give her a huge hug.

"I can only tell you one-hundredth of what happened to me," Ann says in a soft voice. "It is a very long story. I was born in Lublin, Poland, in 1916. At 13, we moved to Warsaw, but when the Germans started building the ghetto, my mother, sister Sylvia, and I fled to a small town called Zwolen. My father and older sister, Temma, stayed behind to take care of our apartment and possessions. Life was easier in Zwolen. We farmed and ate what we grew."

Grandma smells as if she's been cooking chicken soup or her famous chocolate cake. She greets me in her pink, cozy floral robe and asks, "How are you today? How is life treating you?"

"My father died of pneumonia after he and Temma came to join us in Zwolen during the winter. I remained with my mother and two sisters and met and married my husband.

"At this time, some Poles had set up a make-believe camp that Jews paid to go into because if we paid we were protected. We stayed there until the police came. My husband was taken to Buchenwald, and my mother was rounded up with other older people and children. I saw her being marched away and never saw her again. Temma was able to flee to Russia. Sylvia and I were first taken to a munitions work camp in Poland, then another camp for a few months, then suddenly to Germany, to a very terrible camp called Ravensbruck."

Natalie listens intently as her grandmother continues, despite having heard this story many times. "By this time, the Americans were moving closer, so we were moved to another camp farther away. There we were made to go through the clothes of the dead, looking for gold. But here I was lucky. They needed girls to work in the kitchen, and my sister pushed me off my wooden bed, and made me stand and be selected.

"I got all the soup I wanted, and stole pieces of bread that I'd give my sister later in the bathroom. Still, I was hungry all the time and couldn't sleep. When I was a girl in Warsaw, my mother brought in a cup of water and milk to me every morning because I always fainted. But in four years in the camps, when I was always hungry, I never fainted once."

I make my way into the comfortable den with the huge TV and "vege" for a while. Grandma comes in carrying a tray of delicious chocolate cake and a tall glass of cold milk. I sit eating with her arm around me, while I tell her what is going on in my life.

"By then we could hear the Allies dropping bombs, but it didn't bother us at all. We had nothing to lose. The Germans were very scared, though, and made all of us, 700 women, leave the camp. We marched and marched, and one day passed a forest. I was with my sister, two other sisters, and another girl. One of the other sisters, the bravest of us all, said, 'If the SS guard turns his head, I'm running into the forest. Follow me!' Just then he turned his head and she ran. And scared as I was, I ran, too!"

Natalie has moved next to Ann, and lays her head on her grandmother's shoulder. "In the morning we woke up, and a German soldier was standing over us. We all thought we were dead. But he said, 'Don't be afraid, I won't hurt you. The Allies are coming. You'll be liberated.' He explained he'd been ordered back to Berlin, but wasn't going to go. He left and we clung together, hiding all day. The next morning, he appeared again and ordered me to go with him. I thought for sure he was going to kill me now. But I had no choice, I had to go."

Grandma is a good listener. She pays close attention to what I tell her, and offers her opinion. Grandma is wise, experience-wise.

"When we were alone he reached into his jacket, but not for a gun as I thought, but for money! He gave me 20 marks and said, 'You'll need this when you're liberated to buy food.' Then he gave me his mother's address and asked that when I'm liberated to please write to her and say I saw him and that he was well. Then he left and we never saw him again.

"Later, the brave girl went into town and ran back saying there were white flags all over. We walked into town and there were the Americans! They were wonderful to us. They took us to a farm and made the Germans give us the big house where we had a bedroom and a kitchen to ourselves. And do you know, that 20 marks from the soldier was a miracle! I can't tell you how long it lasted, and what we were able to buy with it!"

After watching our favorite shows, I go to bed, turning down the volume until it's just a murmur. I fall asleep quickly, knowing that Grandma is in the next room.

"My husband and sister did not survive Buchenwald. We don't know anything about my 16-year-old brother, or the one in Russia. My second younger sister was okay in Russia with her husband.

"We went to the camps to look for relatives but didn't find any. Then we moved to Stuttgart and found many people we knew. I met my second husband there, and we got married."

I wake up late and there's a breakfast of fresh rolls and fruit. Grandma is dressed in a blouse and slacks, her hair made up and her makeup done perfectly. I tell her I'm not hungry, but she insists I eat anyway.

"My husband's uncle lived in Davenport, Iowa. He'd told his son, who was in the Army, to look for any relatives, and he found us. The uncle, a very good man, brought us and other relatives to America. We worked hard. My husband had been an accountant at home, but here he opened a liquor store and worked day and night."

Ann pauses. The sounds of a late summer's night drift through the open windows. Laughter, music from a car radio, a playful bark. Natalie stretches—it's a school night and tomorrow she has soccer practice. After that, piano.

Ann looks lovingly at her granddaughter and sighs. "The main thing I can't understand is how we all came out of it as normal people. We got married, and had normal children. This I can't understand." Gently, she pats Natalie's head.

When I'm ready to go home, Grandma tells me to put on my sweatshirt. "No," I say, "it's hot out!" When I go outside I shiver. It's freezing! I quickly pull on my shirt, then turn to look up at the second-story window. There I see Grandma. She winks at me. I don't know what I'd do without Grandma. She's my inspiration, my guide, my friend. I love her dearly. I always will.

Frank

Clara Hyde

Bob Brown

"*I* almost divorced him over that!" says 77-year-old Clara Hyde, normally such a pleasant woman that even feigned anger turns her cheeks as pink as her boot-cut pants. "Can you imagine burying all his solid silver trophies in the front yard?"

"Grandpa just figured those trophies were cluttering up the place," laughs Bob Brown, 33, the Hydes' 6-foot-4-inch grandson, who's come to celebrate his birthday at their California horse ranch. "Grandma likes to save all that stuff, but it doesn't mean anything to Grandpa."

While wife and grandson discuss his idiosyncrasies, Frank Hyde relaxes in his easy chair, looking every inch like an American icon. His blue eyes sparkle beneath the brim of his white cowboy hat, his smile is inscrutable on his sun-etched face, and his shiny cowboy boots peek out from his crisp Levi's.

At 80, Frank not only maintains his six-acre ranch unassisted, but is a fierce competitor in the centuries-old tradition of gymkhana. Silver belt buckles, the size of paperback novels, worn by Frank, Clara, and Bob, attest to Hyde's prowess at the daredevil sport that pits horse and rider against the clock as they careen through 12 events in an arena-sized obstacle course. Frank, the most senior rider among 5,800 statewide competitors, always enters the fastest divisions, and has twice been named to the Hall of Fame.

Frank and horses have been a winning combination from his childhood days on a Missouri ranch. "I rode nine miles to school every day," he remembers, "racing other kids each way." It's no surprise then that Bob got his first pony at 4 months.

"Put him on it that same day," Frank says. "Course, I had to hold him."

"I had that pony, Cherokee, until I was 12," says Bob. "He was big and worked

a cart. I remember Grandpa trying to show me how to drive, but I insisted on taking him sidewise and broke the cart."

Did Frank get angry? "Never," says Bob. "Of course, I can remember times when I'd be up on the hay and he'd ride by and give me a look where all the blood drained out of his face. Then I'd think, 'Oh God, Grandpa doesn't want me up here.' But, I never remember him getting angry or scolding us."

How does Frank account for his mild manner? "What good does it do if you get angry?" he shrugs. "Doesn't accomplish anything."

"I've always tried to emulate that," says Bob, whose own easy laughter suggests he's succeeding.

Clara has another insight into her husband's even temperament. "He can get a new ornery horse to train, and I'll watch them at the beginning and think, if I were training that horse, I'd probably want to hit him to make him see who's boss. But Frank never does. He has such patience. At the end of 30 days, he'll have that horse doing just what he wants."

Frank's patience extends to riders, too. After retiring as a dairy salesman, he coached children in gymkhana, running clinics under the relentless sun, then playing tag on horseback with them under the starry sky for recreation. Clara cooked meals in the red barn where the children bunked and used her business acumen to run the program as well as their riding equipment mail-order business.

Like many of their generation, the Hydes have a strong work ethic honed during the Depression. "I knew I didn't want to spend the rest of my life having nothing," Clara says, and Frank agrees. "We started buying rental properties as soon as we were married, and I did all the maintenance on them. By the time we retired, we had them all paid for," he says.

"We were just Depression kids," says Clara, "and hard work and honesty mean everything to us. Why, if Bobby ever took a nickel from anybody, I think I'd disown him."

Bob agrees that his grandparents taught him discipline. "But you always knew they loved you. I felt very spoiled and privileged, having opportunities other kids didn't."

The Hydes wasted no time introducing Bob to their favorite sport. "My sister and I would go with Grandma and Grandpa in their motor home to the state shows," Bob remembers. "Grandma would feed us, then take us to the back to lie down. She'd rub our heads as we fell asleep, and the breeze would blow through the windows. If we came to something of interest, like the Golden Gate Bridge, she'd wake us up to see it." Clara produces a worn, but still colorful, Indian blanket that Bob remembers being wrapped up in while sitting in the stands watching his grandfather perform. "You'd better not have gotten that blanket dirty, though," he recalls, "because Grandma had a temper!"

"Oh, Bobby, I did not!" Clara chuckles.

"Oh, yes you did!" Bob reminds her, launching into a falsetto impression of his grandmother. "We'd be crossing the street, and Grandma would say, 'That's right, now just step right in the grease! Go on! If you're lucky you can get both feet dirty!'"

"Oh, that's not true!" Clara laughs. "You're always making fun of me!"

Fun seems to be the operative word around the Hyde ranch. Despite the arduous work—boarding horses; mowing acres of grass; maintaining barns and tack rooms; and harvesting avocados, nectarines, and grapes—a fringe-topped surrey, right out of *Oklahoma!*, and a life-size stationary white stallion are testaments to the Hydes' humor and whimsy.

Inside the comfortable living quarters, vivid is the main motif. "Friends step into the red living room," says Bob, "and say, 'It's so bright!' I tell them, 'That's Grandma! She's flamboyant!'" Which accounts for the pink carpet in the kitchen and closets of crinolined ball gowns, which Clara wears to Masonic and Eastern Star formals. She and Frank are both high-ranking members, and Bob has joined, as well.

Along with her graceful grandson, Clara enjoys ballroom dancing, an activity about which Bob is passionate. "I was going through a blue period and Grandma gave me a newspaper clipping about free dance lessons. I thought it might cheer me up, so I went," says Bob. "I was watching the lesson when Lily May Warren came over and asked if I'd like to dance. She was a schoolteacher, and knowing her now the way I do, I realize she thought I was a lot younger, because if she knew how old I really was, she'd never have asked me to

dance. But, we turned out to be good partners, and started dancing together." Bob gets that smile on his face that means Clara is about to be teased. "About the third dance I went to, Grandma said she wanted to come along. Lily May said she thought Grandma wanted to check out who I was with."

"Oh, that's not so, Bobby," Clara replies. "I knew Lily May from Eastern Star. Why, she's 81 years old! She's like a second grandma to you!"

For all their good-natured teasing, these grandparents and their grandson are mutually respectful and admiring. "I just hope I can live as long as they have and get along half as well," says Bob. "I've got a certain amount of guilt that I don't get here more often to help with cleaning out the corrals. They never ask, but I should probably take more responsibility."

Neither Clara nor Frank seems to feel that Bob's the least bit remiss. His grandmother produces an oversized Mother's Day card from him enumerating all the positive habits he's learned from her: manners, frugality, straight posture, regular church attendance, and good business sense.

"I was so proud of that card," Clara says. "I took it to the beauty shop and showed it to everybody!"

Not missing a chance for one last tease, Bob says, "Oh, Grandma, did you believe that? Why, it was lies! All lies!"

Grandparents & Grandchildren Camp:

Jim & Kim Maas,

Barry & Ashley Bolden,

Lou Calabro, &

Kevin & Joshua Perez

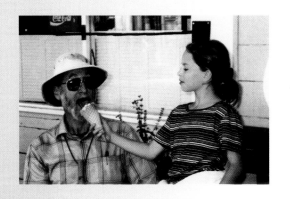

The brainchild of Sierra Club volunteers Jim and Helen Maas, Just for Grandparents and Grandchildren Camp was conceived in 1993. "We were leading an art and hiking outing for adults in the Sierra Nevada mountains," Jim, a retired businessman, college professor, and administrative analyst for the San Francisco Police Department, says, "when we happened to run into an old backpacker friend as he was saying good-bye to his wife and granddaughter. He was going to spend the week on our trip, and they were off for a week at Lake Tahoe. 'Hey,' I said to myself, 'why couldn't they stay here? It would be great to have an intergenerational family around.' Since Grandma already had plans to visit family at Lake Tahoe, off they went. But on the spot, Helen and I decided we were going to try an outing with grandparents and grandkids the following year."

That first season there were 16 participants, including the Maases' 10-year-old granddaughter, Kim. Five days later, when camp was over, Kim eagerly asked, "Can we do it again next year, Grandpa?" and Jim knew he had launched a tradition. Within two years, the group had grown to its maximum capacity of 36 "grand people," as Jim calls his campers. Some return year after year, cherishing their memories of scenic nature trail hikes, sleeping in a rustic lodge, swimming in sparkling mountain lakes, and just getting to know each other better.

Take Lou Calabro, a 30-year veteran of the San Francisco Police Department,

enjoying my grandkids just as they are, and at the same time passing on to them the things that I have learned that actually work in this insane life.

"For the past five years, each Wednesday I pick them up at about 7 A.M. and we have breakfast before I drop them off for school. Sometimes they lock me out of the car, sometimes they hide from me, sometimes they drive me nuts. But I love them and come back for more.

"On this trip, though, Kevin and I had a small breakthrough. He accepted me as the person in charge and realized he had to adhere to my reasonable requests. That took three days. But now he sees me as a different person. A better one, I hope!"

Kevin agrees. In a preternaturally mature observation, the 10-year-old reveals, "Grandpa seemed more sensitive when we were camping."

Surprisingly, although hiking, riding the tram to the top of Squaw Valley, and playing soccer appealed to the boys, their favorite activity was doing chores at the lodge. Each grandparent and grandchild team only had to volunteer for one chore, but Lou's spirited grandsons signed up for four! "We liked scrubbing and rinsing the dinner pots with Grandpa," says Kevin.

"Lou had to pitch in to help them," says Jim Maas, "and he probably wished those boys hadn't had such zeal!"

Lou had mixed feelings. "They were proud of tackling such an immense job, but let me tell you, those pots were big!"

For other campers, like Ashley Bolden, being outdoors made

who attended in 1997 with his two grandsons, Joshua and Kevin Perez. "Five days with two boys, 9 and 10 years old, was quite an experience for dear old Grandpa Lou," the retired lieutenant chuckles. "Did I learn anything? Yes! Patience is essential to the greatest impression. "I thought the country was pretty," the 8-year-old city girl says, "and I liked looking at the wildflowers, which were different than the ones we have at home."

This is exactly what her 58-year-old program engineer grandpa, Barry Bolden, had hoped for. "I wanted to impart to her an appreciation of natural wonders and wildlife. This was her first long-term stay in the country, and our first long-term time together."

"I thought it would be boring," Ashley admits, "because I didn't know anybody. I didn't want to leave home, but my parents said I had already made plans with Grandpa."

"It took no time at all for her to bond with the other kids," Barry says. "I hadn't ever really seen her interact with other children before and I learned that she does it very well. Sometimes she can be a leader, and sometimes a follower." Barry also recognized a similarity in their personalities. "She doesn't sit still a lot," he laughed. "She's very active, like me."

Among Jim Maas' favorite memories is the evening they took the kids to the nearby railroad tracks where an occasional freight or Amtrak train goes by. "We were going to put pennies on the track, which is something many of us older folks used to do when we were younger," says Jim. "We gave the kids pennies, which they unquestioningly placed on the rails. I explained to them that another train might not pass for hours, and that we might have to come back the next morning to reclaim the flattened pennies. Well, about five minutes later, we heard a train

whistle in the distance, and within minutes the coins were properly rolled over. The really fun part of the event for the grandparents was seeing the kids jumping up and down like hyped-up chimpanzees. They were so excited with a simple experience like that...nothing high-tech, no Internet, no violence—except to the coins, that is!"

As a remembrance of their time together, a mutual gift-giving ceremony is held on the last evening. Barry Bolden gave his granddaughter, Ashley, two intact skeet targets that he had found. Ashley reciprocated with a handmade gift, a sachet created out of tea bags and wild flowers wrapped in a napkin. The next day, on their way back to the city, the once-reluctant camper hopefully asked her grandfather, "Can we come back again next year?" The tradition goes on.

Adopt-a-Grandparent

Lafayette Students:

Denise Buerrosse,

Kristin Caliolo,

Allison Crable,

Shayne Figueroa,

Rhonda Grobman,

Jaime Hubert, &

Lynn Moran

Eastwood Residents:

Evelyn Leibenguth,

Sarah Munford, Nicholas

Stebe, & Mary Zukiewicz

*I*t's early evening at Lafayette College, a small, well-regarded liberal arts school nestled in the historic Lehigh Valley of Pennsylvania. Young men and women crisscross the verdant hilltop campus, invigorated by the crisp breeze that forecasts fall's return. They head for the library to begin a new semester's studies, the dorms to catch up with friends, or the dining hall where they'll grab supper.

But for a handful of students, it's time to hop on a van and drive over to Eastwood, a local convalescent home. There, these Lafayette volunteers will be reunited with their "adopted grandparents," a group of senior citizens whom they haven't seen since last spring.

"The students who volunteer for our Adopt-a-Grandparent program have maturity, commitment, and courage," says Sue Ruggles, the indefatigable director of Lafayette's Community Outreach Center. "We've run this particular program for 10 years," says Sue, "and out of the almost two dozen volunteer groups we offer, this is the one where you have to be psychologically prepared to face the possibility that the next time you return, your partner may not be there."

For Jaime Hubert, a major in Spanish and the arts, the benefits of participating in the program outweigh the emotional risks. "I volunteered in a similar program when I was in high school," says the affable senior. "I really enjoy knowing how much our visits mean to residents who don't have any local family who can visit them." She jokingly admits, however, that she hasn't told her own grandparents back in New Jersey about being in the program. "I don't want them to get jealous that I'm seeing these grandparents more often than I'm seeing them!"

Jaime and two other students, Kristin Caliolo and Denise Buerrosse, have been primarily paired with "grandmother" Evelyn Leibenguth, a sprightly, blue-eyed octogenarian who rose from elementary school teacher to principal in the Easton school system.

"Evelyn never married," says Kristin, a junior majoring in American Studies, "but she traveled a lot, and owned a condominium that she really loved. She still talks about one day returning to it." Although Kristin admires her adopted grandmother's career and accomplishments, she has also been with her during painful moments that provoked reflection. "I was with Evelyn last year when she received the news that one of her last surviving friends had died. She was so saddened that she broke down and cried." The experience has stayed with Kristin. "I hope one day I'll have a family of my own," she muses, "but I guess you never know."

"Jaime and I haven't seen Evelyn since last fall," says Denise, a government/law and English major with a 1,000-watt smile. "When she learned we were going abroad last semester, she kidded that she was really jealous. So we sent her a postcard, and Kristin read it to her."

"She enjoyed the card a lot," says Kristin, who cites her love and longing for her grandparents as a motivating factor for her work at Eastwood. "I learned a lot from my grandparents, and I'm also learning from Evelyn, listening to her experiences and finding out about her perspective on things. She told me that she survived breast cancer at the age of 20, and she's quite religious

now. She doesn't get to church, but she has tapes of sermons and listens to them in her room."

For Shayne Figueroa, a buoyant junior from South Carolina, the Adopt-a-Grandparent program helped her get through a difficult emotional time. "I lost my grandmother during my freshman year," she says, uncharacteristically subdued. "I was very close to her and really felt the loss. Volunteering at Eastwood, being able to spend time with older people, really helped me feel better. It's also given me a better understanding of how older people think and feel. Now when I meet them on the outside, they seem more approachable and I'm not afraid to offer help." Later this week, Shayne will spend two hours at Eastwood. This evening she's devoting time to another community outreach program, leading a group of volunteers who teach arts and crafts to needy youngsters.

By the time the students arrive at Eastwood, dinner hour is over, and some of the residents are already upstairs in bed. Several entertain guests in their rooms; some are being wheeled by their visitors down the hallways. One elderly woman cradles a baby brought to the home by his mother, happily showing off her tiny visitor at the nurses' desk.

Rhonda Grobman, a senior who is employed by Sue Ruggles to help recruit and organize students for the program and liaise with Eastwood, finds out that her "grandmother," Margery Trayes, is in bed. Earlier in the day, the 97-year-old former schoolteacher fell and is resting. Rhonda leaves to visit her, while the others head down the hall to the brightly lit activity room.

There, three residents sit before a television set. On the screen is a staff member's home videotape of her little daughter's birthday party. Nicholas Stebe, Ph.D. and former head of a high school math department, dozes. Evelyn Leibenguth—Kristin, Denise, and Jaime's adopted grandmother—and another resident, Mary Zukiewicz, a retired restaurant owner, watch the birthday girl try to smash open a piñata.

"Hi, Evelyn," Kristen and Jaime call out, entering the room. Immediately, the young women's palpable enthusiasm and energy distract Evelyn and Mary from the TV. Even Nicholas is roused. "I remember you," says Evelyn, putting out her hand, which each of her "granddaughters" takes in turn.

For Sue Ruggles it's an affirming moment. "The 'grandparents' really look forward to these visits. They'll tell the volunteers, 'Call me if you can't come.' But everyone always does." Sue recalls one exceptional Lafayette student who forged such a close relationship with his adopted grandparent that he continued to visit him four years after graduating, until the grandparent's demise.

Sue notices that Lynn Moran, a major in chemistry, and Allison Crable, a second-year psychology major, are looking about for their adopted grandfathers. Sue speaks with a staff member, then gently informs the girls that the two men passed away over the summer.

Both girls are shaken by the news, and the other young women come over and comfort them. "I used to visit a man everyone called 'Holmey,'" says Allison. "He had Alzheimer's, and spent all his time sitting in the lounge, where he loved to watch *Oprah*. He wouldn't remember me from one visit to the next, but when I came in he'd always call out, 'Hello, young lady!,' as if he were happy to see me." Remembering him, she smiles.

Lynn allows herself to weep over the loss of Charlie, her "grandfather," whom she remembers as an upbeat Phillies fan who loved to sing and tell jokes from *Reader's Digest*. "I was worried about him before I left last year," the sensitive junior acknowledges. "He was put on new medication, and he just didn't seem to be his old self." Gradually, Lynn and Allison join the others.

The students mingle with the "grandparents," passing a bowl of pretzels, handing Mary a cup of juice. Nicholas beams, surrounded by so many attractive, attentive women—several of them history majors, his old love! The young and the old hold hands, offer hugs and affectionate pats, exchange pleasantries and news, and make plans for future visits. At parting time, they take away a bit of grandmotherly advice from Evelyn: "Don't worry about school. Have fun. See everything that you can!" Her words echo down the hallway, and into the autumn night.

Mary Garofalo

Janeane

Garofalo

Ask Janeane Garofalo how often she gets to visit her paternal grandmother, Mary Garofalo, and the film and television star blurts out a confession as if she's been waiting for the "Grandparent Police" to catch her. "I really love going to see her, I do," she says, "but I just don't get there often enough." Not even trying to cop a plea, Janeane readily admits, "It's all my fault. Totally my responsibility! I'm the one to blame."

On the other hand, Mary, Janeane's only living grandparent, tends to be more sanguine and philosophical about her occasional visits with her celebrity granddaughter. "She's very busy these days, and I understand that. But she calls, and we get to catch up on the phone."

Although all grandmothers would prefer a personal visit, Mary can see her granddaughter on a 40-foot-high movie screen, HBO specials, and Comedy Central shows. Not to mention the framed poster from Janeane's hit film *The Truth About Cats and Dogs*, which Mary displays prominently in her immaculate, memorabilia-filled living room. "My friend asked the video store owner if he'd please give it to her when he was finished with it," Mary explains. "Then, after she got it, she gave it to me." Mary may be a proud grandmother, but she's not pushy.

Nevertheless, in Mary's small New Jersey town, Janeane's success has become a matter of communal interest. The security guard in Mary's building has taken on the role of archivist, taping all of Janeane's cable television appearances for her grandmother. "The only thing that gets me mad at her," Mary says, "is when she doesn't tell me if she's going to be on TV."

Years ago, Janeane, a self-described "high school dweeb," couldn't conceive of herself as a comedic star, despite the fact that her classmates voted her "Class Clown." Before tackling comedy professionally, Janeane graduated with a degree in history from Providence College. There, too, her friends intuited her talent, and she was named "the funniest person in Rhode Island." When she was 20, she began doing stand-up, still her first love, despite having concerns about the level of good comedy at most of the traditional clubs.

After college, Janeane worked as a bicycle messenger in Boston. "My goal then was simple. I thought I'd become a secretary. That was about the limit of my fantasies." But for people like Mary Garofalo, who knew Janeane as a child, it was clear that being around people and making them laugh were always what Janeane loved best. "I remember going to my son's house to visit, and Janeane was always about to run off to be with her friends. So one day," Mary recalls, "I said to her, 'You know, I'm your friend, too!'"

This truism is not lost on her granddaughter, who, as a kid, conceived a crazy plan to unite the doting Mary with her lenient maternal grandfather. "My mother's parents were Irish, and my Irish grandmother was very strict. But her husband was a real pushover. My Italian grandfather was a disciplinarian, too, and didn't let us get away with a lot. So I imagined it would be so cool if my sweet Italian grandmother could marry my sweet Irish grandfather. God, can you imagine what my brother, sister, and I could have gotten away with?"

Although Mary's husband may have been strict, Janeane does remember sneaking into his candy drawer during her family's regular Wednesday and Saturday visits. "We scored all kinds of hard candies and chocolates," remembers Janeane, proclaiming Mary's house to be "Food Central." "We'd just sit around all day and stuff our faces. My grandmother's an incredible cook—everything she makes is amazing!"

Mary mastered the art of cooking the same traditional way that her eight brothers and sisters did. As each turned 12, they were required to spend time in the kitchen and apprentice with their mother. "We all had to learn, although it was more important for the girls, since they'd have to cook one day for their husbands," Mary says. "The one thing I never learned how to make of my mother's," she adds regretfully, "is her homemade macaroni. I remember her putting flour, eggs, and water on the table, and never even measuring them."

Even without macaroni, Mary's list of amazing dishes makes it difficult for Janeane to choose a favorite. "Just pick one? That's hard. They're all so incredible. But, okay, if it has to be one, I guess I'd have to go with her escarole soup." That recipe was handed down from Mary's immigrant grandmother with whom, as a small girl, she'd spend two weeks each summer on the family farm. Mary doesn't remember much about those visits, except there being lots of fruit trees, "and having to pick up lots of apples."

Today, the regular Wednesday and Saturday visits from her grandchildren are gone. With Mary's three children, 10 grandchildren, and seven great-grandchildren scattered around the country, she more than appreciates whatever time she has with them—especially during the holidays.

"Holidays?" Janeane asks. "Holidays? Does my grandmother make a deal over the holidays? What month is it now? July? I'm telling you, she's already finished shopping for Christmas! She lives for Christmas. You can't believe how many presents she used to give us. There were Hefty bags filled with them!"

Mary remembers a Christmas, however, when Janeane felt she was getting less than she deserved. "She got mad because her sister got more boxes than she did," says Mary. "And I had to explain to her that it wasn't the number of boxes that you got, because some things will cost more than others. I think she understood."

That was not the only life lesson that Janeane learned from Mary. Another was respect. "My grandmother is a devout Catholic, so there are areas that I don't go into in my act," says Janeane, whose outspoken, irreverent humor has led to her being described by one reviewer as "the stealth comedy weapon in any movie." "I know she'll see me, and I don't want her to ever be offended. It's out of respect for her that I keep certain things to myself."

Mary's impact on her granddaughter has been personal as well as professional. When asked what's the most important way in which Mary has influenced her, Janeane answers without hesitation. "This might sound strange coming from me," she says, "because I don't have any yet, but, definitely, it's my love for kids. I think I'm really good with them, just like my grandmother. I know I definitely want to have kids!"

When Mary is asked to name one wish she has for Janeane, she, too, is able to answer quickly. "A child," she replies. "I want her to have a child."

And what is Janeane's response to learning of their common goal? "My grandmother said she wishes that I have kids? Wow! That makes my day!"

Mary Garofalo's Escarole Soup

First, make either chicken or beef broth.
Then boil escarole in salted water. When done,
squeeze out the water thoroughly.
Chop up the escarole and add it to the broth.

P.S. If using beef broth, add tiny meatballs.
Count out 100, so if anyone asks,
you can tell them that's exactly
how many are in there!

Charlene

George Boller

Kristi Stone

risti Stone races down the track, her long, slim legs kicking up clouds of dust behind her. "That girl's like a human spring!" her maternal grandfather, retired fireman George Boller, quips. As the 11-year-old sprints between the guide ropes scoring the field at the Braille Institute Youth Center—where track events are held for young people, like Kristi, who suffer from visual disabilities—George watches in sheer admiration. "What an amazing child," he says. "I can't tell you how proud I am of her!"

Kristi's pretty blond grandmother, Charlene, echoes her husband's thoughts, then adds a maternal postscript. "If I had given birth to Kristi, I would have spoiled her, instead of treating her like everybody else."

But, on at least two counts, Kristi Stone *isn't* like everybody else. First, she was born with a rare form of blindness, Leber's Congenital Amaurosis, which robbed her of her peripheral vision, and left her able to see only well-lit objects in extremely close proximity.

And second, Kristi Stone is a perfectionist. "I'm kind of competitive," says the young girl who consistently sets, and achieves, goals that exceed those of many peers blessed with normal eyesight. Out of 30 in her sixth-grade class, Kristi was one of two students awarded gold certificates by the President's Fitness Council; she has also successfully competed in both the Burbank and Braille Institute Olympics, where her specialty is the standing long jump.

 Her accomplishments aren't only on the playing field, however. For receiving all A's and B's in fourth and fifth grades, Kristi won a Presidential Academic Award. "If I mess up on my homework, I throw it away and start over," she says matter-of-factly, despite the fact that reading and writing are laborious for her.

"Every day, an instructor from the Braille Institute spends one hour with Kristi in class," says Charlene. "Since fourth grade, she's been receiving instruction on how to use a Braille stylus, which is a sort of typewriter that translates into Braille. But a while ago, she told me she wanted to give it up. This wasn't unusual, since she's always resisted using special aids that she thinks set her apart.

"So I sat her down and we had a little talk. I told her I thought she was fortunate to learn how to use the stylus, because many people lose vision later in life and have never learned how to read Braille. Also, she might be able to use her skill one day to help teach others."

With her tenacity and courage, Kristi *is* a natural role model and teacher. Her grandmother, whom Kristi calls Char, gave up waterskiing several years ago after suffering a mishap. She was coaxed into giving it another try this past summer, however, when Kristi decided to take up the sport herself, despite being unable to see the boat that would pull her or the direction in which it was going.

"Kristi thought she would get up the first time," says George, whom Kristi calls Papa. "She got really angry when she didn't. She can be very hard on herself, not realizing that other people have trouble, too."

"But it all worked out," Charlene says. "Kristi succeeded, as usual, and we had a wonderful time. I'm so glad that she inspired me to try it again."

Kristi has also inveigled her grandmother to take up rollerblading, which they do together when she visits with her active, athletic grandparents at their desert vacation home. "When I'm there I like going on the golf cart with Papa," Kristi says, punctuating her statement with an infectious giggle. "We play cards, too—War and Crazy-8s." After a pause, she admits graciously, "Char usually wins."

"Kristi brings out that spirit in me," her grandmother chuckles, reaching out to caress her granddaughter's silky straight hair. "Do you want to tell what we do when you sleep over?" she asks. At first, Kristi just giggles, but then gives in to the coaxing.

"They make me a princess bed," she says.

"We set it up in our bedroom, next to our bed..." says Charlene.

"With piles of quilts and comforters," Kristi adds.

"Then she makes believe she's asleep, don't you, Kristi? And in the morning she'll tell us everything we've said, word for word!" says George.

"She's got an amazing memory. At school, when the teacher writes on the chalkboard, she'll say out loud what she's writing so Kristi can write it down quickly," explains Charlene. "A lot of the time, though, Kristi just memorizes what the teacher says, then when she gets home, she sits down with her mother and writes everything out. At night, it's not unusual for her friends to call her and ask, 'Kristi, what did the teacher say we were supposed to do?'"

Everyone has a good laugh at that. A decade earlier, however, there was little to smile about regarding Kristi's disability. "When she was about 3 months old, her mother and I knew something was wrong," says Charlene. "She wasn't tracking normally, not the way her two older sisters did. But my daughter and I wouldn't say the word to each other," she says.

Shadows are Kristi's enemies, as well as unseen obstacles out of range of her extremely limited vision. "As she's grown up, there have been so many times when she's banged into things and really hurt herself," says George. "But she's never wanted pity, never wanted to show how much it hurt. She just wants to be treated like everyone else."

And so she is. When Kristi announced during a family camping trip that she wanted to learn to ride a two-wheeler *without* training wheels, her father, who, like his father-in-law, is also a firefighter, helped her on a bike, then gave her a push. "I knew he was watching, holding his breath," says George, "as Kristi struggled to keep her balance going over all those dirt bumps. Every now and then, her father would yell out, 'Tree!' and Kristi would turn the bike the other way."

"It's hard sometimes not to be afraid for her," says Charlene, reaching out to squeeze Kristi's hand. Kristi smiles back at her, as if to reassure her grandmother. "Sometimes we've watched her and been real afraid, but then we sit back and look at her mother and her father, who are okay with it, and because they're with her all the time, we follow their lead."

"I hold my breath when I watch her rollerblade," says George. "I don't know how she does it. She zooms down her driveway, and somehow knows to make that sharp right turn onto the sidewalk. She's remarkable!"

Six years ago, George and Charlene moved from their home across the street from Kristi's to a beach community some three hours up the California coast. "We come down to Burbank at the drop of a hat, though!" says Charlene, whose four children and 12 grandchildren live within 20 minutes of each other.

"Almost every other month, we try to get everybody together to celebrate the birthdays for those two months. Plus there are always things going on with the grandkids that bring us into the city," says George.

On this sun-filled day, Charlene takes Kristi's right hand, George her left, and the three stroll across the Braille Institute's wide green lawn. Kristi, "the human spring," bounces as she walks. You can almost hear her thoughts. She's heard of something interesting that she wants to try—beep ball. "She wanted to play baseball," says George. "But Charlene talked with her and explained how even people with normal eyesight can get hit by the ball, so it's probably not the best sport for her."

But beep ball, the Braille Institute's version of baseball where sound guides the players to find the ball and the bases—now, that's interesting! Kristi giggles. It looks like she just might have found her next challenge!

Esther Rettinger,

Naomi Attie,

Ceil Fisher

Mark

Nancy Cole

Loeterman

"*L*et me help," says each of the three grandmothers as Nancy Loeterman covers her patio table with a pretty vintage tablecloth. "That was mine," says Ceil Fisher, smoothing down a corner, then admiring the refreshments her grandson, Mark, serves. So what if everyone's just returned from brunch? There's always room for a glass of iced tea or a plump summer fruit.

"Ceil and I have been best friends for 60 years!" Esther Rettinger says, beginning to explain the dynamic of this extraordinary family. At 94, Esther's hearing is diminished and she walks with a cane, but her vibrant voice recalls the strength of her younger years, when she worked with her husband at their butcher shop. Ceil picks up the story.

"Esther was already in California when I moved here from New York. Another family introduced us, and we've been friends ever since!" Ceil ("GG" to her grandchildren and great-grandchildren) looks remarkably robust and relaxed only weeks after open-heart surgery. "I call Esther three times a day, just to see how she's doing," Ceil says. She holds a bright green envelope containing the birthday card Esther gave to her over brunch. This week, Ceil turns 87. "Can you imagine, in 60 years we've not had one problem!" What neither woman imagined at the beginning of their friendship was that Ceil's daughter would one day marry Esther's son, and the two women would bond through marriage as well as friendship.

Now enter Naomi ("Nan") Attie, a gracious woman, whose sculpture wins prizes at local art shows. She is about to turn 90. A good friend of Esther's and Ceil's, she is also united with them through marriage: Her granddaughter, Nancy, is married to Esther and Ceil's grandson, Mark.

159

Mark and Nancy Loeterman, a warm, handsome couple in their early 40s, appreciate the uniqueness of their extended family. "We have three grandmothers who enrich our lives in so many ways," Mark says. "It's wonderful."

The Loetermans, both busy attorneys and parents of two active children, do more than just talk about their good fortune—they integrate their grandmothers in all aspects of family life. Today they've gathered to celebrate Ceil's birthday. In a few weeks, the family will attend a gala dinner honoring Nan's 50 years of community service.

"But anything is an excuse for us to get together," Ceil chuckles.

"I think it was the grandmas who worked to include Nancy and Mark at the beginning," Nan says. "It was up to us to keep the family together. There was the telephone, of course, and on Friday nights we always had dinner at my house."

"I really think that Nan's *Shabbat* dinners are what held us together, especially when I was young. [Shabbat is the traditional Friday night meal that marks the beginning of the Jewish Sabbath.] Everyone in the family came, not because we had to, but because we wanted to. Everyone had something interesting to say, and it was a way to catch up on everybody's news," says Nancy.

"And don't forget we traveled together, too," Nan adds.

"Oh, we went on great trips together!" Nancy remembers. "Nan and my grandfather, Eli, took us to Hawaii, Russia, and Israel."

"There'd be 18 of us traveling together," says Nan. "It was just wonderful."

Mark's experience with his grandparents was as memorable and binding as Nancy's. "Every Sunday was open house," says Esther. "Anybody who was hungry could come over. Later, when Ceil was a widow, she'd come, then Mark and Nancy came every Sunday like clockwork. Mark would run up the driveway yelling, 'Oh, Grandma, I can smell the chicken soup already!' Recently, I have to depend on someone to take me places, so I'm always happy to go and see all the children. I have eight grandchildren, and umpteen great-grandchildren! They all call me 'Bubba Esther.'"

Ceil especially enjoyed the six months that Mark lived with her while at UCLA. "He was a joy!" she says.

"What else can she say?" Mark laughs.

"No, I mean it!" Ceil says. "You know how young people tell you they'll come home at nine o'clock, but they never do. Well, when Mark would say it, he'd by home by nine!"

"Maybe our kids should hear this!" Nancy jokes.

Ceil gazes fondly at her grandson's wife. "When he married Nancy," she says, "it was the joy of our lives!"

"And Ceil is always there for us," Nancy says with equal affection. "It's the same with Nan. All of Nan's grandchildren come to her with their problems. She'll cook breakfast for us and give out great advice. With Ceil, if Mark and I are in a fight, all I have to do is call her up and ask, 'Tell me if I'm right or wrong.'"

"And she's always right!" says Ceil.

"And I'm always wrong!" laughs Mark.

How do Mark and Nancy explain their special bond with their grandmothers? "This relationship is different than the one we have with our own parents," says Mark. "We can confide in our grandmothers, discuss things with them, and get a different perspective. So this relationship is very special in that way."

The grandmothers also enrich the lives of Mark and Nancy's children, Leah and Jacob. Nancy recalls the first time they brought their newborn daughter to a Shabbat dinner at Nan's. "There must have been 16 people there, and when we brought her in, everyone gathered around us, and handed her from person to person."

"We're very fortunate because we live close to each other and see each other no less than once a week, and talk several times a week," Mark says. "We probably see Esther a little less frequently because she lives farther away. But when we do visit, the children really enjoy themselves. Esther has books from when she was a young girl in Hebrew school. Our kids love to look at those books and read out loud to her. And she very much enjoys listening to them."

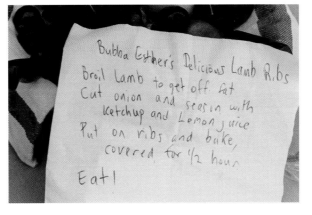

Bubba Esther's Delicious Lamb Ribs
Broil Lamb to get off fat
Cut onion and season with
Ketchup and Lemon juice
Put on ribs and bake,
covered for 1/2 hour
Eat!

Asked if she still can read Hebrew, Esther answers emphatically. "Of course! I can't go to temple anymore, but I do the Friday night service at home, from beginning to end, and the Saturday service, too. The fact that I can't go to temple doesn't hold me back."

"They all have such a strong belief in God," Nancy says.

"Nancy," Mark asks, "do you remember the time we were at Nan's house for one of the High Holy Days, and we were playing a game, asking questions like, 'If you were on a desert island, what would be the one thing you'd need to have?' And of maybe three dozen people around the table, the grandmothers all gave the same exact answer. They all said they would need to have their faith in God. It was so interesting that they all believed the same thing."

Mark and Nancy wish to emulate their grandmothers' faith, resilience, independence, and tolerance as they continue with their lives. "They are the most nonjudgmental people I know," Nancy says.

"You get a little wisdom as you get on in years," Nan chuckles.

"Yes, you get wisdom when you're older," agrees Ceil. "Especially if you don't get bored! Nan is always busy with her art and charity work. I keep busy reading and being with my friends. When you're older you can't be a complainer. If people ask me how I feel in the morning, I always say, 'I'm making it!' You have to go on and live every day like it's the last."

With that, Nan pulls out a bag of homemade chocolate chip cookies from her large purse and offers them around the table to her good friends and grandchildren. "I always have a little something with me," she says, smiling.

The giving never ends.

Annie Abcarian

Robin Abcarian

As a tribute to her late grandmother, newspaper columnist and talk show host Robin Abcarian wrote the following extraordinary essay, which was published in the *Los Angeles Times*.

HER ONLY EXTRAVAGANCE WAS HER LOVE OF FAMILY

My indomitable grandmother, Annie Abcarian, died last week. She was 92 years old, and in death, as in life, she surprised. I'd expected something awful at the end—stench, rot, ugliness. But on her deathbed, she was sweet-smelling, white-haired, and lovely. She looked like a tiny, toothless angel. Strokes had stolen her tongue, but when I kissed her forehead, she smiled.

"I love you, Grandma. Just let go."

"Pretty eyes," she said.

She was human glue, my grandma was, keeping her three sons and nine grandchildren as close as she could, reminding us over and over that family matters most of all. A provincial view, maybe, but the legacy I treasure most.

My grandma was small and stocky and amply endowed with hair a tad too blue on occasion, a sense of humor about her dentures, and a near complete lack of interest in fashion. If it wasn't polyester—that is, if you couldn't put it through the wringer and dry it under the relentless Fresno sun—she wasn't interested. She wore simple A-line shifts, even weeded her tomatoes and waxy peppers in them. She would snazz up her wardrobe with hand-crocheted vests. By the end of her life, nearly everything she owned was covered by something she had crocheted: beds, couches, tables, armrests, rolls of toilet paper. She never did crochet the bikini I'd requested. Probably just as well.

She was thrifty, too, absurdly so. She saved a chewed-up half stick of Doublemint on the bed stand in a tiny plastic box, her "gum garage." The pace at which my siblings and I went through paper towels, the fact that we stood in front of an open refrigerator door for more than five seconds, gave her fits.

When she moved from Fresno to the Armenian retirement home in Los Angeles a decade ago, we discovered stockpiles of toilet paper in her closets—a lifetime supply, bought by the bushel on sale. You would expect this, I suppose, from an immigrant who grew up poor, who always worked, who never allowed herself to be pampered, spoiled, or seduced by the acquisitive ethic of her adopted country.

And yet she was strangely commemorative about the things she owned. Each chair, each couch, each TV set had, in some secret place, a piece of masking tape with the date of purchase and price noted in ink. Toward the end, she'd add the name of one of her heirs. She'd already decided who'd get what.

She died, just as my father had predicted, on the last day of April, getting her full month's rent worth from the nursing home.

My grandmother was part of the Diaspora, coming here from Armenia (Turkey, actually, but she'd kill me if I said so) early in the century as a young child. She missed the horrors of the genocide, but she was surrounded by people who had not, including my grandfather, and like them never spoke of what she knew or had heard. For many Armenians, the wounds were too ghastly, too close to the bone to risk reopening with talk.

She keenly felt any loss suffered by her family. You could tell by how she looked. But out loud, her fatalism kicked in. "That's okay," she'd say of divorce, miscarriage, car accidents, rejection slips. "Why dwell on it?"

It was a family trait. "Well," said 90-year-old Great-Aunt Martha at her sister's funeral, "it can't be helped."

Fatalism implies an acceptance of one's preordained place in the universe—for my grandmother, an arranged marriage, children, the life of a housewife. It wasn't enough. To my grandfather's horror, she insisted on going to work after the farm failed. She spent years on an assembly line, on her feet, packing dried figs for pennies and a tiny pension. When my grandfather died at 58, my grandmother was only 47. She became self-sufficient, leaning on no one, never remarrying. And she bloomed into an iron-willed matriarch.

At 77, she insisted on driving cross-country with me, from California to Florida. All the way, she barked orders and lifted the tips I'd left for waitresses if she felt I'd been too generous.

"Men are animals," she told us gravely when we were in high school. By college, though, she took me aside. "Don't get married right away. Live together first. Just in case."

After I married, she would sit at my dining room table, rolling grape leaves for *sarma*, impressed by my non-Armenian husband, who slyly explained he'd acquired his rolling skills with a different sort of leaf.

"That's okay," she'd say.

"Hey, Grandma," we'd tease. "How do you say 'far out' in Armenian?"

The love she gave was not always appreciated. She could be bossy and intrusive. But in the end, it came back to her. During the last days, my father and his brother kept a vigil at her bedside, holding her hands, stroking her forehead, telling her she was loved. I have never witnessed such tenderness by grown men.

We buried her Saturday in Fresno next to my grandfather, Mike. He's been saving the space since 1952. It was in the poor people's part of the cemetery, right next to the road. Traffic was so loud at times we couldn't hear the priest.

But what a deal! My grandma paid $300 for the double plot in 1952. Today's price: $1,200.

Her journey through life was a modest one, lacking grandeur and sophistication. She had no great expectations, just a great passion for her family. That may not seem like much of a world to some, but for my grandmother, it was the universe.

Cecil B. DeMille

Cecilia DeMille

Presley

"From the time that I could dress myself, Grandfather took me everywhere with him when he traveled," says Cecilia ("Cece") Presley, describing one aspect of the amazing relationship she shared with the legendary film director and producer, Cecil B. DeMille. "Whether it was Egypt to make *The Ten Commandments*, or simply to a speech in Chicago, he took me along."

One of their most memorable trips took place almost half a century ago, when she and DeMille traveled across America with the Barnum & Bailey Circus in John Ringling North's private railroad car. DeMille, wanting to make a circus picture, made the trip as part of his usual extensive research. "Of course, being 13, I fell madly in love with the circus," says Cece. "Then, one day, Grandfather said, 'Look, Pet, you're supposed to be *helping* me, but every time I need you, you're on the trapeze, or riding an elephant, or playing with the lions!' He really did look to me for advice. In fact, I was one of the few people who'd tell him when I thought something was terrible." The circus story was made, and in 1952, *The Greatest Show on Earth* won the Academy Award for Best Picture of the Year.

Sometimes when they traveled together, moviemaking wasn't the only thing on their agenda. "Traveling with Grandfather was so special," says Cece. "At Valley Forge he'd talk for hours about the founding of America and freedom, or in some exotic place he'd tell me about the world's great religions, which he studied throughout his lifetime."

One Christmas in New York, Cecilia recalls DeMille sending her on a shopping spree for toys, explaining they'd be sent to children who had written to him. "I asked why he was doing this, and he said, 'Because Santa Claus is having a hard time coming to their homes.' It was typical of him to make a point with an illustration, not a lecture."

Sitting in her elegant living room, surrounded by priceless artwork from DeMille's early movie posters and leather-bound manuscripts from his extensive personal library, Cecilia recounts her grandfather's philanthropy with pride. "Someone once called our family 'the artists, the givers, and the doers,'" she says. "I don't mean this as a boast; it's just the kind of life we had. It was instilled in us to make the world a better place. If you believe that, then you have to do something about it." Today, Cecilia runs the DeMille Foundation.

Cecilia's exceptional closeness with her grandfather began at the family compound. "Mother, my stepfather, and I lived in a house next door to the 'big house,' which belonged to Grandfather and Grandmother," says Cece. "We'd go there every night for dinner and to screen a movie. I spent so much time with Grandfather as a toddler that we just bonded. Mother was always close with him and worked with him in the business, as did the rest of the family. She didn't mind when Grandfather turned the anteroom into a room for me, and I began to stay there. She was a very good mother, and I always had a room at her home, but Grandfather just took over raising me."

Being raised by DeMille meant exposure to fascinating people, places, and experiences. "I remember, during the Second World War, listening with Grandfather to one of FDR's Fireside Chats. The president talked about a Navy doctor, Corey Wassell, and the crew he was caring for on Java. These men were too badly injured to be put back on ships returning to combat. A decision was made to leave them for the Japanese. But Wassell heroically risked moving the men to the other side of the island, where they managed to catch a Dutch freighter and get to safety." For most listeners, FDR's talk was just a good story, but for DeMille it was the basis of a movie. "Grandfather and I went to the studio the next day, and he said to his secretary, 'Get me the president.' Well, FDR came to the phone, and they talked for a few minutes. Then Grandfather said, 'Mr. President, I'd like to borrow Corey Wassell.' The president replied, 'I'd give you the Navy, Mr. DeMille, but they're a bit busy right now. But Corey Wassell will be right there!'" Cecilia's life lesson from this high-level eavesdropping? "When people know that you're doing good, you have tremendous power."

DeMille's power was most evident on a movie set, where, even Cecilia admits, he could be dictatorial. "When he began shooting a picture, everything changed! Nothing else mattered! Unless you make major motion pictures, you have no idea of the logistics. It's huge! Once shooting starts, you're on a schedule and being one day over can mean hundreds of thousands of dollars. So, if an extra talks when he's not supposed to and ruins a shot, it's a disaster. Because of that, he was a total tyrant on the set!"

But when shooting was over and life at home got back to normal, "the tyrant" was ruled by his wife, daughter, and cook. "If he was told to sit down and have dinner, he did," chuckles Cece. "He was a fabulous raconteur, and we had wonderful people to the house all the time: Yul Brynner, Jimmy Doolittle, Billy Graham, Sam Goldwyn." And how does a child relate to such icons? "We were carefully listened to, but when you weren't amusing anymore, you were excused. And, of course, if you weren't amusing often enough, you weren't asked back!"

Did she ever keep a journal about those days? "I did once," she says ruefully. "When we went off traveling, I hid it in the eaves of the attic, not knowing that Grandfather planned to remodel that space. When we returned, I found the carpenters reading my diary, hysterically laughing at everything I'd written. That was the end of my journal-keeping!"

But that certainly wasn't the end of Cecilia's experiences, as she continued to learn from her grandfather. "Grandfather directed *Lux Radio Theater,* a very popular program, and earned a good deal of money doing it. But when the American Radio Guild demanded that all union members pay one dollar towards a campaign fund for a politician whom Grandfather didn't support, he refused to pay. So they took him off the air. Hundreds of people volunteered to pay for him, but he refused. I asked him, 'Grandfather, why are you fighting this? You're losing so much money!' He turned to me and said, 'Because, Cecilia, I have to shave every morning!'" Eventually, the Supreme Court handed down a precedent-setting decision that no union could assess a member for political causes.

DeMille was pro-union by choice. Some of the union members, like the crew with whom he worked continually from 1913 to 1956, were treated to his generosity when he made them beneficiaries of a share of the profits from *The Ten Commandments* for the remainder of their lives. "I still make out checks to these people," says Cecilia, abiding by her grandfather's legacy of honesty and loyalty.

Today, Cecilia passes on these same values to her own grandson, Travers, 12, with whom she travels, climbs mountains, goes white-water rafting, and enjoys literature, art, and music. She finds in Travers some of the same qualities that she believes drew DeMille to her when she was a child. "I think a lot of grandparents are energized by the children they care for. And it's also the innocence. If you've lived long enough, you've seen a lot of bad stuff in the world, especially if you're in a difficult business like the movie business. There's something wonderful about the innocence of a child, the ability to take that child and mold his mind with stories and experiences."

It didn't take adulthood to impress upon Cecilia how unique her upbringing was. Even as a child, she knew that her life was exceptional. "I remember one night, when I was about 10, walking across our property. I stopped in the rose garden and sat down on a bench and said to myself, 'Remember *every* day!' It was all so special, and I was *so* lucky to be a part of my grandfather's life."

Florence Campbell

&

Kelsie Daniels

"*I* definitely got my work ethic from Grandma!" declares 28-year-old Kelsie Daniels, recently voted New York City's top fitness trainer by *Allure* magazine. Before dawn, Kelsie's already working out with the first of her eight daily clients—jogging, lifting weights, and scouring food diaries for nutritional no-no's.

"And I'm always out of the house by 6 A.M.!" states Florence Campbell, Kelsie's grandmother, and owner/operator of a school bus service. A youthful 67, Florence concedes that transporting kids makes for "a long, stressful day," but she, like her svelte granddaughter, clearly thrives on hard work.

"I don't know if Grandma ever said it out loud," says Kelsie, "but she certainly implied, 'Work for yourself! Be your own boss. If you don't take care of yourself, no one else will!' She gave me the idea to start my own business!"

Florence frowns. It's a sore spot between them that Kelsie never completed college, but what can you do when your words come back to haunt you? "She's always been trouble," Florence teases.

"Me?" Kelsie giggles, before confessing to some childish mischief when she lived with Florence after her parents' divorce. It was during this time that grandmother and granddaughter forged the strong bond that they share today.

Even their few differences prove to be negotiable. For example, Florence is a collector. "It's nice to be able to look back and see the things you've felt were important during your life," she says. Kelsie, on the other hand, boasts, "I throw everything out, and when I do, I think of her!"

And while Florence had three children, her granddaughter has only recently entertained the idea of one day becoming a mother. "If I do have kids," Kelsie muses, "I know I'll save all the memory things, and wind up being exactly like Grandma."

Russ Barry

Russell

Ryan Barry

"What's the difference between fathering and grandfathering?" Russ Barry, a veteran television executive, ponders the question as he gazes at photos of his children and grandchildren adorning the desk and walls of his Warner Bros. Studio office.

"Well, the most striking thing is time. I had Michael [Russ' eldest son, who turns 40 this year] when I was really young. I'd just turned 20. At the beginning, I spent a reasonable amount of time with him, but then it trailed off. By the time my first three children were born, I was living in Connecticut, working in New York, and commuting three hours a day. After a long week at work, the weekend would come and I'd think, I really want to play golf, and so that's what I would do." He pauses. "There were always a lot of ways to be distracted."

A man who's come to terms with his past, Russ responds forthrightly and unapologetically. Divorced from his first wife, he's spent the last decade building solid relationships with his three older children (two sons and a daughter) and entering a second marriage that produced daughter Shannon.

"Being a grandfather," he continues, "you don't have the time element imposed on you. You're a friend. You don't have the real responsibility, the accountability of how the kids are brought up." He shows off a beguiling photo of his two grandsons, Russell, 9, and Ryan, 5, who live in Indianapolis. In the picture, they're frolicking in Russ' swimming pool, perched on the broad shoulders of their dad, Michael.

For many years, Russ admits, he and Michael didn't know each other well. "I remember when he was in high school and one summer took off on a camping trip in a beat-up old van with his girlfriend. While they were away, this young woman, out of the blue, wrote Michael's mother and me a letter all about him, saying that she wanted us to really know what a terrific person our son was." Russ' voice breaks slightly. "It was striking. It really opened my eyes."

Years later, father and son now share several bonds. One of them is fatherhood, and some lessons that a father learned from his son. "Michael is such a wonderful father. He's so attentive to the boys. Work and home, maybe going to the gym once in a while, that's his whole life. Although we're father and son, we pretty much talk as equals now. Being a grandfather to his children reinforces everything about our own relationship." If Russ thinks his own fathering skills were lacking early on, where does he think Michael learned his? Russ answers candidly, "I'm sure some of it is thinking, 'I'm never going to do that!'"

Being so introspective about his past has resulted in Russ Barry's priorities being more clearly defined now. "It upsets me that the boys are so very far away. There are big gaps of time that I don't see them, and phone conversations don't always make it. Russell's in the 'yup/nope' stage, and Ryan's still too young to carry on a conversation for long."

That's why family vacations, when Russ' and Michael's families get together, are so eagerly anticipated. Every Christmas they go skiing together, and over the summer they meet for a week filled with sports, Lego building, and games of Battleship. This past summer they rented a house in Michigan, so Michael and his family could drive up with all their sports equipment.

When Russ travels for business to the East Coast, he routes himself through Indianapolis to spend a few days with the boys. "It's not an easy connection, but I always try to do it," he says.

Although he's fit and energetic, it's daunting to imagine the times when Russ is being simultaneously sought after by two active grandsons and a toddler daughter. "It all works out," he chuckles. "Shannon's their aunt, but they don't really get it, yet. She's just 'baby Shannon' to them. Russell's very sweet with her. He picks her up and carries her around, and then, of course, occasionally drops her. But she's great with them, not jealous at all of my paying attention to them. It's as if she knows I'm her Daddy and also their Pop. Of course she wants to do everything they do, like swim in the pool or go to Disneyland. But we manage to work it out."

If one thing is evident about Russ Barry's relationship with his children and grandchildren, it's that he has put time, thought, and energy into "working it out." Now comfortable and happy in the dual roles of father and grandfather, he looks forward to getting even closer to the youngest generation. "Russell's very adept at the computer," he says proudly. "He's way ahead of me. He leaves me there—it's a real disconnect—a cultural, generational thing. But I just bought a computer and I'll catch up." He smiles. "Then we can e-mail!"

Acknowledgments

Love and gratitude to Gerry, Tracy, J.J., and Katie for creating my life's fondest memories.

- C. A.

A hug for my husband, Stan, whose love always sustains me.

- F. M.

Our thanks to Nessa Cooper for her friendship, intuition, and generosity, which initially brought us together. To Quay Hays, Publisher, and Peter L. Hoffman, Editorial Director, thank you for "getting it" the first time we met. To all at General Publishing Group, Inc., especially Sharon Hays, Marc Nobleman, Carmen Pascual, Lori Rick, Trudihope Schlomowitz, Chitra Sekhar, Mina Silverstone, and Dana Stibor, much appreciation for your tireless efforts and collaborative spirit. And deep gratitude to countless friends and colleagues who provided invaluable ideas and encouragement.

Our special thanks to Robin Abcarian, Leslie Avayzian, Noa Ben-Artzi, Sherri Cooper, Jean Craig, Samuel Hartman, and Natalie Schachner for granting permission to publish their copyrighted works. And for their cooperation and assistance, we are grateful to Leah Rabin, Elizabeth Brown at the Library of Congress, Karla Crawford at the Foster Grandparent Program, the Washington State Apple Commission, and the Dwight D. Eisenhower Library.

Finally, to all the gracious and hospitable grandparents and grandchildren who shared their homes, hearts, and memories with us, thank you for making us feel "part of the family."

Photo Credits

Thank you to the following contributors for providing family and/or archival photographs and artwork:

Page 17: Courtesy of Jerry Orbach
Page 19: Courtesy of Jerry Orbach
Page 24: Drawing by Larry Keams
Page 28: Courtesy of Don Bond
Page 29: Courtesy of Don Bond
Page 39: Courtesy of Leslie Avayzian
Page 48: Courtesy of Carol Burnett and Erin Carlson
Page 49: Courtesy of Carol Burnett and Erin Carlson
Page 51: Courtesy of Carol Burnett
Page 53: Courtesy of Samuel Hartman
Page 60: Courtesy of the Dwight D. Eisenhower Library
Page 63: Courtesy of the Dwight D. Eisenhower Library
Page 76: © Tim Wood
Page 79: © Tim Wood
Page 96: Courtesy of the Queen family
Page 99: Courtesy of the Queen family
Page 103: © E. O. Hoppé
Page 114: AP/Wide World Photos
Page 117: AP/Wide World Photos
Page 126: Courtesy of the Stengel family
Page 129: Courtesy of the Washington State Apple Commission
Page 142: Courtesy of Lou Calabro
Page 143: Courtesy of the Maas family
Page 144: Courtesy of Lou Calabro
Page 145: Courtesy of Barry Bolden
Page 169: Courtesy of Cecilia DeMille Presley
Page 172: Courtesy of Cynthia Barry